The
End of the
Cold War

Titles in the World History Series

WORLD
HISTORY SERIES ■■■

The
End of the
Cold War

by
David Pietrusza

Lucent Books, P.O. Box 289011, San Diego, CA 92198-9011

Library of Congress Cataloging-in-Publication Data

Pietrusza, David, 1949-
    The end of the Cold War / by David Pietrusza.
        p. cm. — (World history series)
    Includes bibliographical references and index.
    ISBN 1-56006-280-0
    1. Cold War—Juvenile literature. 2. World politics—1945-
—Juvenile literature. [1. Cold War. 2. World politics—1945-]
I. Title. II. Series.
D842.P565   1995
909.82—dc20   94-11568
                                                      CIP
                                                      AC

Contents

Foreword

Each year on the first day of school, nearly every history teacher faces the task of explaining why his or her students should study history. One logical answer to this question is that exploring what happened in our past explains how the things we often take for granted—our customs, ideas, and institutions—came to be. As statesman and historian Winston Churchill put it, "Every nation or group of nations has its own tale to tell. Knowledge of the trials and struggles is necessary to all who would comprehend the problems, perils, challenges, and opportunities which confront us today." Thus, a study of history puts modern ideas and institutions in perspective. For example, though the founders of the United States were talented and creative thinkers, they clearly did not invent the concept of democracy. Instead, they adapted some democratic ideas that had originated in ancient Greece and with which the Romans, the British, and others had experimented. An exploration of these cultures, then, reveals their very real connection to us through institutions that continue to shape our daily lives.

Another reason often given for studying history is the idea that lessons exist in the past from which contemporary societies can benefit and learn. This idea, although controversial, has always been an intriguing one for historians. Those that agree that society can benefit from the past often quote philosopher George Santayana's famous statement, "Those who cannot remember the past are condemned to repeat it." Historians who ascribe to Santayana's philosophy believe that, for example, studying the events that led up to the major world wars or other significant historical events would allow society to chart a different and more favorable course in the future.

Just as difficult as convincing students to realize the importance of studying history is the search for useful and interesting supplementary materials that present historical events in a context that can be easily understood. The volumes in Lucent Books' World History Series attempt to present a broad, balanced, and penetrating view of the march of history. Ancient Egypt's important wars and rulers, for example, are presented against the rich and colorful backdrop of Egyptian religious, social, and cultural developments. The series engages the reader by enhancing historical events with these cultural contexts. For example, in *Ancient Greece*, the text covers the role of women in that society. Slavery is discussed in *The Roman Empire*, as well as how slaves earned their freedom. The numerous and varied aspects of everyday life in these and other societies are explored in each volume of the series. Additionally, the series covers the major political, cultural, and philosophical ideas as the torch of civilization is passed from ancient Mesopotamia and Egypt, through Greece, Rome, Medieval Europe, and other world cultures, to the modern day.

The material in the series is formatted in a thorough, precise, and organized manner. Each volume offers the reader a comprehensive and clearly written overview of an important historical event or period. The topic under discussion is placed in a broad, historical context. For example, *The Italian Renaissance* begins with a discussion of the High Middle Ages and the loss of central control that allowed certain Italian cities to develop artistically. The book ends by looking forward to the Reformation and interpreting the societal changes that grew out of the Renaissance. Thus, students are not only involved in an historical era, but also enveloped by the events leading up to that era and the events following it.

One important and unique feature in the World History Series is the primary and secondary source quotations that richly supplement each volume. These quotes are useful in a number of ways. First, they allow students access to sources they would not normally be exposed to because of the difficulty and obscurity of the original source. The quotations range from interesting anecdotes to far-sighted cultural perspectives and are drawn from historical witnesses both past and present. Second, the quotes demonstrate how and where historians themselves derive their information on the past as they strive to reach a consensus on historical events. Lastly, all of the quotes are footnoted, familiarizing students with the citation process and allowing them to verify quotes and/or look up the original source if the quote piques their interest.

Finally, the books in the World History Series provide a detailed launching point for further research. Each book contains a bibliography specifically geared toward student research. A second, annotated bibliography introduces students to all the sources the author consulted when compiling the book. A chronology of important dates gives students an overview, at a glance, of the topic covered. Where applicable, a glossary of terms is included.

In short, the series is designed not only to acquaint readers with the basics of history, but also to make them aware that their lives are a part of an ongoing human saga. Perhaps they will then come to the same realization as famed historian Arnold Toynbee. In his monumental work, *A Study of History*, he wrote about becoming aware of history flowing through him in a mighty current, and of his own life "welling like a wave in the flow of this vast tide."

Important Dates in the History of the Cold War

1914	1920	1925	1930	1935	1940	1945	1950	1955

1914
World War I begins.

1917
Russian Revolution; Czar Nicholas II is overthrown; Treaty of Brest-Litovsk takes Russia out of World War I.

1918-1920
Russian Civil War.

1919
Soviets invade Poland.

1921
Lenin begins New Economic Policy.

1924
Lenin dies; Stalin begins consolidation of power.

1928
First five-year plan begins.

1929
Trotsky is exiled.

1939
Hitler-Stalin pact; Germany triggers World War II by invading Poland.

1940
Trotsky assassinated; Baltic states are incorporated into Soviet Union.

1941
Hitler invades Soviet Union.

1945
Allied leaders meet at Yalta; World War II ends; Tito becomes leader of Yugoslavia.

1946
Dimitrov takes control of Bulgaria.

1948
Yugoslavia expelled from Cominform; Communists gain control of Hungary; Soviets begin Berlin blockade.

1949
German Democratic Republic proclaimed; People's Republic of China is established.

1950
Korean War begins.

1953
Stalin dies; riots in East Germany; Korean War ends.

1955
Warsaw Pact is formed.

1956
Khrushchev denounces Stalinism; rioting in Poland; Hungarian uprising.

1958
Khrushchev becomes Soviet premier.

1959
Castro seizes power in Cuba.

1961
Communists erect Berlin Wall.

1962
Cuban missile crisis and U.S. naval blockade of Cuba.

1963
President Kennedy is assassinated.

1964
Khrushchev is ousted by Brezhnev and Kosygin.

1968
Czechoslovakia's Prague Spring is crushed by Soviet invasion; disturbances erupt in Poland.

1970
Riots break out in Poland; Solzhenitsyn wins Nobel Prize for literature.

1973
First volume of Solzhenitsyn's *Gulag Archipelago* is published abroad.

1974
Solzhenitsyn is exiled from Soviet Union.

1975
Sakharov wins Nobel Prize for peace.

1976
Committee for the Defense of Workers' Rights is founded in Poland.

1977
Charter 77 is founded in Czechoslovakia.

1978
Karol Wojtyla of Poland becomes Pope John Paul II.

1979
Soviet Union invades Afghanistan; Solidarity movement begins in Poland.

rity is recognized as an inde-
ent trade union.

elski crushes Solidarity union;
a is imprisoned.

ncv dies; Andropov becomes
leader.

ient Reagan proposes Strategic
ise Initiative (Star Wars) as part
. arms buildup;Walesa wins
Prize for peace.

pov dies; Chernenko becomes
leader.

enko dies. Gorbachev becomes
leader, initiates glasnost and per-
a, ends placement of SS-20 mis-
Europe; Yeltsin becomes general
ry of the Moscow Communist
ommittee.

obyl nuclear disaster occurs;
chev invites Sakharov to
to Moscow.

chev dismisses Yeltsin from
litburo.

1988
Ethnic violence in Nagorno-
Karabakh region of Soviet Union;
Soviet troops begin leaving
Afghanistan; Kádár ousted in
Hungary; Brezhnev and Chernenko
posthumously stripped of all honors.

1989
Gorbachev renounces Brezhnev
Doctrine; Solidarity again legalized
in Poland; its members win elections
for parliament; Hungary opens border with Austria; Hungarian
Communist party abolishes itself;
Yeltsin wins seat in Soviet parliament; East Germany lifts travel
restrictions between East and West
Berlin; Havel becomes Czech president; Ceausescu is overthrown and
executed in Romania; Soviet Union
completes withdrawal from
Afghanistan; Zhivkov is ousted as
Bulgarian leader.

1990
Opposition parties are allowed in
Soviet Union; All non-Russian
republics declare independence;
Germany is reunited; Baltic states
and Ukraine declare independence
from Soviet Union; Soviet control of
religion ends; Gorbachev receives
Nobel Prize for peace; Walesa
becomes Poland's president;
Slovenia and Croatia form noncommunist governments; first Albanian
opposition party is formed; Yeltsin
heads Russian republic.

1991
Soviet Union recognizes indepen-
dence of Baltic states; coup against
Gorbachev fails; Soviet Union is dis-
solved; Gorbachev resigns;
Commonwealth of Independent
States is formed.

1992
Gamsakhurdia is ousted in Georgia;
Berisha becomes first noncommunist president of Albania; Iliescu is
reelected president of Romania; former communists regain power in
Lithuania.

1993
Czechoslovakia splits into Czech and
Slovak republics; Yeltsin storms
Russian parliament and ousts hard-
liners; former communists return to
power in Poland; new Russian constitution passes; Zhirinovsky
becomes force in Soviet politics.

1994
Former communists regain power in
Belarus; candidate favoring return to
Russian rule wins presidency in
Crimea.

A History of Distrust

For seven decades beginning in 1917, mistrust and rivalry existed between the communist government of the Union of Soviet Socialist Republics and the noncommunist world. Communists believed their system would eventually destroy and replace capitalism. "We will bury you," threatened Soviet leader Nikita Khrushchev.

Nikita Khrushchev summed up the animosity between the United States and the Soviet Union when he declared, "We will bury you."

Because such animosity dominated Soviet policy, the United States and its allies attempted to block Soviet expansion, calling their policy containment. It included diplomacy, foreign aid and, occasionally, armed conflict. From Korea to Vietnam to Cuba's Bay of Pigs, the cold war occasionally turned hot. Thousands of nuclear missiles were poised to destroy all human life on earth if the order came from the White House or the Kremlin. The threat of nuclear warfare hung like a giant sword over the planet. Stakes were very high, indeed.

The story of the cold war, however, cannot be told just in terms of foreign policy, missiles, or military actions. While it existed, Soviet communism seemed indestructible. Whenever a Soviet satellite nation started to break away, Soviet tanks would roll in, crushing the rebellion. In the Soviet Union itself, organized opposition seemed impossible. The Communist Party controlled almost every aspect of life, including the arts. "One of the major principles is that Soviet literature and art must be inseverably linked with the policies of the Communist Party," declared Khrushchev, as quoted by Gilbert Seldes.[1] The Soviet Union was the first modern totalitarian state, and it outlasted the ones that were later established in Nazi Germany and fascist Italy. An end to communism—except in a nuclear holo-

To the amazement of the world, the Soviet Union's hold over international affairs began to unravel at breakneck speed. A statue of Lenin is dismantled in the Soviet Union in 1991.

caust, which would have destroyed all civilization—seemed almost unthinkable.

Yet in the 1980s the entire Soviet system unraveled. Remarkably, this happened with relatively little loss of life. Even more incredibly, the changes came not from the most oppressed members of society, but from the very top. General Secretary of the Soviet Communist Party Mikhail Gorbachev saw that communism was not working. In order for it to survive, he knew changes had to be made. Gorbachev began policies of glasnost (openness) and perestroika (restructuring) to open up the Soviet Union. He promised to root out stagnation, corruption, and inefficiency.

While doing this, however, he inadvertently unleashed Eastern European citizens' decades of resentment, longing for freedom, and desire for a better life.

Communism had promised a workers'

paradise. It did not deliver one. Under communism, living standards lagged far behind those in the capitalist West. Goods and services were in short supply. Housing was scarce and poorly built. Medical care was free but inadequate. Pollution poisoned the earth. The peoples of Eastern Europe wanted a complete change in how they were governed.

Breaking Away

In 1989 nation after nation broke away from Soviet rule. Poland, East Germany, Czechoslovakia, Romania, and Bulgaria all saw dreams of real independence come true. Then the Baltic states of Latvia, Lithuania, and Estonia broke away. In August 1991 those who opposed Gorbachev's reforms attempted an unsuccessful coup

People in republics that had been under the iron hand of the Soviet Union for decades, such as these Lithuanians, began to revel in their new-found independence.

against him. It failed completely, resulting not only in the plotters' imprisonment but in the sweeping away of the Communist Party and the Soviet Union itself.

Reformer Boris Yeltsin took control of Russia. Many new nations such as the Ukraine, Georgia, Belarus, Armenia, and Azerbaijan were formed. The future seemed bright for those who had suffered for so long.

Unfortunately, economic problems continued. Living standards actually worsened as nations attempted to make drastic reforms in their economies. Old ethnic hatreds reignited. The ethnic populations of Yugoslavia, Georgia, Armenia, Moldavia, and Azerbaijan clashed in bloody fighting. Along with the fighting came fears of what might happen to nuclear weapons stationed in such places as the Ukraine and Belarus.

In some nations, such as Poland and Lithuania, former communists again led governments. In Russia former communists and ultranationalist extremists offered themselves as solutions to their nation's problems. The coup plotters were freed from prison.

In Eastern Europe the present, as well as the future, seemed clouded by massive difficulties, and it was easy to lose sight of

what the end of the cold war meant. Political prisoners had been freed. Thousands of nuclear warheads were dismantled. Millions no longer served in armies poised to destroy each other. Hundreds of millions were now free to speak their minds or worship as they pleased. They now had a glimmer of hope that their lives would someday be far, far better.

Those were major accomplishments. That they were achieved without warfare and largely without bloodshed was all the more miraculous.

Gorbachev went from leader of the world's second most powerful nation to being forced out of office. Despite his personal disappointment, he could claim a great deal of satisfaction from the changes he had set in motion, as this excerpt from his memoirs in *Time* magazine indicates:

Power is transitory, and it's not the best thing to have. Power as such, as "the supreme value" . . . well, I wouldn't have wanted that. I could give it all up. There is another mission: to revive this country, this land that contains a vast world—long suffering, tormented and demoralized—to bring it back to normal life, and to restore to its people a feeling of human dignity.[2]

1 The Establishment of Communism in Eastern Europe

For most of the twentieth century the communist economic and political system ruled over Soviet Russia. Based on the teachings of nineteenth-century philosopher Karl Marx, Marxism/communism

Karl Marx predicted that adherence to his theories would lead to a new world where all people would be equal and taken care of by a benevolent state—but in reality his ideas led to widespread misery.

promised all people equality. Oppressed workers and peasants would live better than ever. In reality, communism led to an elite class that ruled over the people. Freedoms were crushed; corruption was common; living standards lagged behind those in the West.

Marx believed his ideas would first take root in such advanced nations as Germany or England. Yet in 1917 backward, rural Russia saw Marxism's first trial.

Several special conditions helped communism get its start in Russia. The first was the brutal world war that began in 1914. It killed 1.7 million Russians and wounded nearly 5 million more. By early 1917 Russia had grown weary of war and was about to collapse. Its people were desperate and wanted radical change. Russia's Marxists promised the sharpest break with the past.

In 1905, after a disastrous war against Japan, Russians had demanded more freedom. During World War I an absolute monarch, Czar Nicholas II, led Russia. He allowed some reforms and even created a parliament, or Duma. But as tensions eased, he backtracked and eliminated the Duma's political power. With no democratic opposition allowed, Russians turned to the more radical choices offered by the Marxist rebels.

On the Eve of Revolution

Rumors of a Leninist coup were widespread. Frank Golder's Documents of Russian History, 1914–1917 *notes that on the day the Bolsheviks seized power, the newspaper* Izvestiya *(later an official Communist Party organ) sent this too-late warning to the people of Russia:*

"The Bolshevik uprising, if successful, will bring on a series of civil wars between different regions of the country, as well as in the interior of each region. We would have a regime of fist-right. In one place there would be a white terror and in another a red terror. All constructive work for any length of time would be impossible. One of the outcomes of the anarchy would be that the first adventurer to come along would seize power, and the ignorant masses (of whom the country has so many) would turn to Nicholas II to save them from the revolution, which was not able to give the people what it had promised.

The Bolshevik uprising can only lead to that. Is it possible that people do not understand that dictatorship and terror are not the way to organize a country? Is it not clear that dictatorship of one party, no matter how radical, will be as hateful to the great majority of the people as the autocracy? Is it not clear that an attempted uprising, at the time of the preparation for the election to the Constituent Assembly, can be regarded as a non-criminal act only because it is a mad act?"

We Do Not Believe in Eternal Morality

Among those opposing Nicholas II were two Marxist parties, the Bolsheviks and the Mensheviks. Vladimir Ilich Lenin, a brilliant revolutionary attorney and author, led the hard-line Bolsheviks. Leon Trotsky opposed Lenin's elitist theories, which held that the people themselves could not be trusted to transform society. Lenin's ideas would place a highly disciplined, dictatorial party at the head of Russia's revolutionaries. Trotsky led the more democratic Mensheviks, who encouraged greater dissent and discussion. Aided by its very radicalness and ruthlessness, the Bolshevik idea ultimately won. Bolsheviks were rigid, conspiratorial, and centrally controlled. To them the ends justified the means. Lenin regarded whatever aided his cause as moral. He once wrote: "When people talk to me about morality we say: for the Communist, morality consists entirely of compact united discipline and conscious mass struggle against the exploiters. We do not believe in eternal morality."[3]

As Nicholas's regime collapsed, neither Lenin nor Trotsky was actually in Russia. Lenin had been arrested for revolutionary activity in 1895. In 1900 he left Russia for Western Europe. There he set up *Iskra (The Spark)*, a newspaper designed to be smuggled back into Russia to ignite the radical awareness of Russia's common people. By 1917 he was living in Zurich. Trotsky was in New York; he had left Russia after living in Siberian exile following the Russian unrest of 1905.

Lenin returned in 1917 with the help of Russia's German enemies. They thought his presence could disrupt the already fragile Russian society even further. The Germans placed Lenin on a sealed railway car bound for Russia. Germany's ambassador to Denmark, Count Brockdorff-Rantzau, explained, as quoted in Alexander Solzhenitsyn's *Lenin in Zurich*:

> We must now definitely try to create the utmost chaos in Russia. To this end we must avoid any discernible interference [such as openly favoring one side or another] in the course of the Russian Revolution. But we must secretly do all we can to aggravate the contradictions between the moderate and the extreme parties, since we are extremely interested in the victory for the latter, for another upheaval will then be inevitable, and will take forms which will shake the Russian state to its foundations.[4]

With sickening wartime losses and increasing food shortages in the cities, the Russian people wanted radical change. In March 1917 angry strikers in Petrograd (St. Petersburg), the nation's capital, chanted:

Leon Trotsky, head of the Menshevik party, believed that the Russian people, not an elite group of leaders, should be trusted to run the country.

> Out of the way, obsolete world
> rotten from top to bottom.
> Young Russia is on the March![5]

So it was. Even the most hopeful revolutionaries expected the czar's troops to quickly end the strike, but no such thing happened. Russia's rulers no longer had the will to survive, and protest snowballed. Soon Nicholas II abdicated in favor of his brother, Grand Duke Michael. When Michael refused the crown, the three-hundred-year-old Romanov dynasty came to an end.

What would replace it? A temporary government under moderate socialist attorney Aleksandr Kerensky took charge. He placed Nicholas and his family under arrest.

Kerensky believed in political democracy, but he continued the unpopular war against Germany. Thousands of Russians died each week. The nation stood on the brink of economic ruin. These facts alone were enough to doom his government.

Kerensky faced the opposition of a virtual rival government. The Bolshevik-dominated soviets, or workers' councils, controlled city halls in both St. Petersburg and Moscow. Under the slogan "Peace, Land, and Bread," the soviets appealed to war-weary soldiers, landless peasants, and city dwellers angry with chronic shortages. It was a powerful combination.

Hail the Return of Lenin!

In July 1917 a violent Bolshevik uprising rocked Petrograd. It failed, and Lenin went into hiding. In September, Gen. Lavr Kornilov, commander of the Russian army, tried to seize control. To stop Kornilov, Kerensky turned to the Bolsheviks for help and gave them new credibility. Soon afterward Lenin's supporters won clear majorities in both Moscow and Petrograd local elections. Lenin was now aided by Trotsky. On his return to Russia, Trotsky, because of his desire to overthrow Kerensky, had joined the Bolsheviks. Lenin and Trotsky now eagerly attempted another coup.

On the night of November 6–7, 1917 the Bolsheviks seized power. Trotsky announced their triumph to a cheering All-Russian Congress of Soviets of Workers' and Soldiers' Deputies:

In the name of the War-Revolutionary Committee, I announce that the Provisional Government no longer exists. (Applause.) Some of the Ministers are already under arrest. (Bravo.) Others soon will be. (Applause.) The revolutionary garrison, under the control of the War-Revolutionary Committee, has dismissed the assembly of the Pre-Parliament [Council of the Republic]. (Loud applause. "Long live the War-Revolutionary Committee.") . . . The railway stations, post and telegraph offices, the Petrograd Telegraph Agency, and State Bank are occupied. . . .

In our midst is Vladimir Ilich Lenin, who, by force of circumstances, had not been able to be with us all this time. . . . Hail the return of Lenin![6]

Victory was hardly a sure thing for Lenin's Bolsheviks. The war dragged on, and numerous enemies remained. Trotsky proved invaluable in solving both problems. He negotiated peace with Germany. The Treaty of Brest-Litovsk surrendered huge portions of Russian land to the Germans—and guaranteed the ill will of Russia's former allies (the United Kingdom, France, and the United States). Soon the West would halfheartedly intervene on Russian soil.

The Bolsheviks also faced many opponents within the country. Right-wing armies were formed, and a civil war erupted. Non-Russian nationalities such as the Ukraini-

ans, the Baltic peoples (Latvians, Estonians, and Lithuanians), Poles, Georgians, Armenians, and Finns broke away.

Trotsky, a man with no military background, created the powerful Red Army. One by one he conquered all the Bolsheviks' opponents, except for the Baltic states, the Poles, and the Finns.

The Outstanding Mediocrity

In 1921 Lenin added to his power with the aid of the New Economic Policy (NEP). The NEP retreated from Marxist beliefs of state-controlled property. This stabilized the economy, brought Russia prosperity, and gained valuable time for Lenin's regime. Time, however, was one thing Lenin personally did not have. His death in January 1924 set off a bitter power struggle between Trotsky and the colorless, but still highly dangerous, Commu-

Bolshevik troops storm the winter palace during the Russian Revolution that ended the monarchy of Nicholas II.

When Vladimir Lenin died in January 1924, a bitter power struggle ensued between Trotsky and Stalin.

nist Party's general secretary, Joseph Stalin. The brilliant Trotsky was no match for the Georgian-born Stalin, a former seminary student who had robbed banks for the Bolshevik cause. Unlike Trotsky, Stalin was not a great speaker or writer. He did, however, control the party machinery, placing his allies in key positions and freezing out his opponents. His crafty and ruthless cunning gave him powerful advantages over Trotsky, who observed:

> Bureaucracy as bureaucracy is impregnated through and through with the spirit of mediocrity. Stalin is the most outstanding mediocrity of the Soviet bureaucracy. His strength lies in the fact that he expresses the instinct of self-preservation of the ruling caste more firmly, more decisively and more pitilessly than anyone else.[7]

By 1929 Stalin, aided by Lenin's old allies Grigory Zinovyev and Lev Borisovich Kamenev, took control. That same year he forced Trotsky, who had done so much to assist Lenin in seizing and keeping power,

into exile. In August 1940 Stalin ordered Trotsky killed; in Mexico City, an assassin drove a pickax into Trotsky's head.

Stalinism

Stalinism now began. In April 1929 the Communist Party Congress ousted anyone in either the party or the government who had ever opposed Stalin. At the same time the Soviets' war against religious liberty increased. Soviet officials had grudgingly tolerated some freedom of belief. Marxism was an officially atheistic doctrine, and Karl Marx had scoffed at religion as "the opiate of the people." A May 1929 amendment to the Soviet constitution, however, made the teaching of religion a crime against the state. It denied civil rights to clergy. Hundreds of churches closed. In attempting to destroy Russia's religious roots, the Soviet Stalinists even abolished the seven-day week. Henceforth, the work week would consist of four days, followed by a day of rest. This lasted until 1940.

Central planning was at the heart of Stalinist economics. The state would control all industry. Five-year plans, initiated in 1928, set out ambitious goals to double industrial production, particularly in terms of steel and hydroelectric power. Stalin felt rapid industrial progress was essential for the survival of the Soviet state against its foreign enemies. As quoted in Basil Dmytryshyn's history of the Soviet Union, Stalin contended:

> It is the jungle law of capitalism. You are backward, you are weak—therefore you are wrong; hence, you can be

A Totally Different Kind of Bolshevik

Joseph Stalin's background hardly inspired confidence. He participated in a series of armed robberies to further the cause. Despite Stalin's eventual triumph, Trotsky had little respect for him. He wrote in The History of the Russian Revolution:

"Stalin was a totally different type of Bolshevik, both in his psychological makeup and in the character of his party work: a strong, but theoretically and politically primitive, organizer. Whereas Kamenev as a publicist stayed for many years abroad with Lenin, where stood the theoretical forge of the party, Stalin as a so-called 'practical,' without theoretical viewpoint, without broad political interests, and without a knowledge of foreign languages, was inseparable from the Russian soil. Such party workers appeared abroad only on short visits to receive instructions, discuss their further problems, and return again to Russia. Stalin was distinguished among the practicals for energy, persistence, and inventiveness in the matter of moves behind the scenes. Where Kamenev as a natural result of his character felt 'embarrassed' by the practical conclusions of Bolshevism, Stalin on the contrary was inclined to defend the practical conclusions which he adopted without any mitigation [softening], whatever, uniting insistence with rudeness."

Joseph Stalin was a murderously cruel man who eliminated any person of any rank who stood in his way to achieving absolute power.

beaten and enslaved. You are mighty—therefore you are right; hence we must be wary of you. That is why we must no longer lag behind. . . . We are fifty or a hundred years behind the advanced countries. We must make good this distance in ten years. Either we do it, or we will be crushed.[8]

(Right) After the revolution, Stalin seized private lands, making them into large, state-controlled collective farms. This strategy led to massive food shortages.(Bottom) Collective farmers start out for the fields to begin spring planting. State-controlled farms led to the Great Famine, in which ten million Russians died.

Collective Farms

In the countryside Stalin forced farmers onto great kolkhozes, or collective farms. In the 1920s many farmers owned their own land. Stalin made them live and work on large state-controlled farms. In doing so, he waged class warfare against well-to-do peasants (kulaks), as he did against others who had prospered under the old order. Anyone who had done well before the coming of the Bolsheviks was assumed to have exploited his fellow citizens. "What does this mean?" Stalin asked about his policy. He answered his own question: "It means that after a policy that consisted in limiting the exploitative tendencies of the kulaks, we have switched to a policy of eliminating the kulaks as a class."[9] Their land would be taken from them. Many were imprisoned. In the Ukraine Stalin's policies of seizing land and destroying incentives created the Great Famine. Ten million died. Stalin did not care. "For Stalin the peasants were scum," said future

While much progress was made, the reality of the five-year plans was not as rosy as Soviet propaganda stated. Very often industries merely faked production figures and turned out poor-quality goods to meet too-ambitious goals.

Soviet leader Nikita Khrushchev, who worked closely with him; "He had no respect for the peasants or their work."[10]

The Communist Party's turn came next. In December 1934 Stalin ordered the murder of popular Leningrad party leader Sergei Kirov. That triggered the Great Purge in the party. Stalin trusted no one and purged one million party members. By 1939, 98 of the 139 Central Committee members elected in 1934 had been shot. Stalin even arrested such old Bolshevik leaders as Zinovyev and Kamenev, who falsely confessed to plotting to kill Stalin.

These starving orphans represent a tiny portion of the massive suffering and widespread hunger that affected all of Russia with the seizure of private lands and the development of collective farms.

No such plot ever existed except in Stalin's mind.

Western observers were shocked by the Stalin Show Trials, in which former Communist Party officials were placed on trial and declared their involvement in conspiracies that never existed. Many of those confessing were such ardent Stalinists that if General Secretary Stalin wanted them to be traitors, they would gladly admit to *being* traitors. The party meant more to them than their own lives.

"We are not like other people," admitted Yuri Pyatakov, a former party member executed in 1938:

> If the party demands it, if it is necessary or important for the party, we will be able by an act of will to expel from our brains in twenty-four hours ideas that we have held for years. . . . Yes, I will see black where I saw white, or may still see it, because for me there is no life outside the party or apart from agreement with it.[11]

Such was the twisted logic of a system relying on ever-greater fear and terror.

Stalin also began eradicating suspected opponents in the Red Army. Some estimates say he purged thirty-five thousand officers. His victims included Russian Civil War hero Marshal Mikhail Tukhachevsky, who was executed in June 1937.

In March 1938 a purge of the Right Opposition (those who had opposed collectivization in 1929–1930) began. Nikolay Bukharin (former editor of *Pravda*, the official paper of the Communist Party, and leader of the Comintern, the organization responsible for world communist revolution) was among those found guilty. Prosecutors falsely accused defendants of

The 1939 Hitler-Stalin pact allowed Adolf Hitler (addressing German masses) to invade Poland and begin his attempt at world domination.

conspiring with German and Japanese agents. Even former NKVD (secret police) head Genrikh Yagoda, charged with poisoning famed novelist Maksim Gorky, was executed. Decades later his guilt or innocence in Gorky's death remains a mystery.

We Would Have Been Invincible

Throughout the 1930s Stalin's Soviet Union and Hitler's National Socialist (Nazi) Germany were bitter rivals. On August 23, 1939, these two former archenemies became allies, signing the infamous Hitler-Stalin pact, or the German-Soviet Nonaggression Pact. On its face the treaty merely said that neither nation would wage war against the other. As quoted in Dmytryshyn's history, the pact reads, in part: "The two contracting parties undertake to refrain from any act of violence, any aggressive action and any attack on each other severally or jointly with other Powers."[12] But an additional secret agreement was included: Germany and the Soviet Union would divide Poland. Stalin could also grab the Baltic states, Finland, and part of Romania.

The treaty allowed Hitler to invade Poland in September 1939, thus triggering

the horrors of World War II. On June 22, 1941, Hitler double-crossed Stalin. His armies rolled across the Russian border, reaching to within twenty miles of Moscow (by now the Soviet capital) and almost surrounding Leningrad (the former Petrograd).

According to Mikhail Heller and Aleksandr Nekrich, authors of a history of the Soviet Union, Stalin's daughter, Svetlana Alliluyeva, later said of her father's reaction to Hitler's treachery:

> He had not foreseen that the pact of 1939, which he had considered the outcome of his own great cunning, would be broken by an enemy more cunning than himself. This was the real reason for his deep depression at the start of the war. It was his immense political miscalculation. Even after the war was over he was in the habit of repeating, "Ech, together with the Germans we would have been invincible!" But he never admitted his mistakes.[13]

Great Britain, which was already fighting Germany, and the United States arranged for aid of large amounts of war materiel—equipment and supplies—to the Soviets. Later the Western Allies opened up several new fighting fronts (in North Africa, Italy, and France) against the Nazis. By May 1945 Hitler was defeated. But the price of victory was huge for the Soviet Union: 6,115,000 dead and 14,012,000 wounded.

During the war some Westerners who had previously distrusted the Soviet Union let down their guard. They did not want to question the methods of an ally that had suffered millions of casualties in fighting Hitler's Germany. At Yalta, a town on the Black Sea, in February 1945 American president Franklin D. Roosevelt and British prime minister Winston Churchill met with Stalin to discuss the future of postwar Europe. They accepted the Soviet dictator's word that he would allow free elections in Eastern Europe, but the West soon found out how worthless Stalin's promises were.

People's Democracies

As the triumphant Red Army swept westward defeating Hitler's armies during World War II, it forced new communist regimes on nation after nation. If left to themselves, Eastern Europeans would almost certainly have voted for noncommunists rather than for Stalin's local allies who stood for repressive dictatorships and selling out their countries to the Soviet Union.

The Smallholders' Party, which represented small farmers, won free elections in Hungary in November 1945. For three years a coalition led by Zoltán Tildy ruled. In 1948, however, the Soviets, in control of all Hungarian military forces, imposed a communist government on the country. They arrested the leader of the Smallholders' Party and made him falsely confess to trying to overthrow the government. The communists threatened their opponents and rigged elections. Mátyás Rákosi's communist People's Democracy seized private farms, factories, and businesses. Throughout Eastern Europe the Soviets repeated this pattern of seizing power, choking dissent, and centralizing the economy.

Czechoslovakia, which had been conquered by Nazi Germany before World War II, was reborn after Hitler's defeat. A communist-dominated coalition government surrendered the eastern portion of the country, Ruthenia, to the Soviet Union. Soviet-inspired violence included the throwing of Foreign Minister Jan Masaryk to his death from a balcony in 1948.

Poland's borders shifted westward. The Soviet Union kept the territory given to it by the Hitler-Stalin pact. In return Poland received Danzig, (Gdansk) Silesia, and part of East Prussia from defeated Germany. Communists began taking power in Poland as early as 1944, as they followed the Red Army back into their homeland. In 1947 it appeared that the noncommunist Peasant Party would win elections. Stalin ordered the Peasant Party's phones cut off and forced its leader, Stanislaw Mikolajczyk, to flee the country. Rigged voting gave control to long-time communist Wladyslaw Gomulka. According to author Norman Davies, Stalin knew what little support Gomulka's followers had, telling one of them: "When the Soviet Army has gone, they will shoot you like partridges."[14]

After the Soviets signed an armistice with Romania in September 1944, local noncommunists were forced out of political life, and a communist-dominated government was forced on Romania in 1946. After King Michael abdicated on December 30, 1947, local communists proclaimed yet another people's republic and

In violation of the Hitler-Stalin pact, German troops invade Russia in 1941. Stalin always remembered the betrayal with shock, believing that together, Russia and Germany could have taken over the world.

subordinated their country's interests to that of the Soviet Union.

On September 5, 1944, the Soviet Union invaded Bulgaria. Four days later local communists seized power. By December 1947 long-time communist Georgi Dimitrov had consolidated a Soviet-style dictatorship and adopted a constitution based on the Soviet Union's.

The Iron Curtain Descends

Some areas were forcibly brought into the Soviet Union. Freed from Nazi oppression, the Baltic states were made part of the Soviet Union. A portion of the German province of East Prussia was annexed to the Russian Soviet Federated Socialist Republic, the largest of the Soviet Union's republics. The Soviets deported many natives and brought large numbers of ethnic Russians into each republic.

After World War II Germany and Austria (which had been part of Hitler's Third Reich) were divided into Soviet,

American, British, and French zones of occupation. In September 1949 the western areas of Germany became the Federal Republic of Germany. Stalin responded by forming the German Democratic Republic (GDR), or East Germany, in October 1949. Unlike democratic West Germany, Stalin's puppet East Germany allowed little freedom and no opposition.

In Albania the leader of the guerrilla National Liberation Movement, Enver Hoxha, installed a communist government in 1944. In Yugoslavia, Marshal Josip Broz Tito, wartime leader of anti-Nazi partisans, won elections in 1945, but only because the opposition monarchists did not take part.

By March 1946, with Soviet-style governments installed in nation after nation, former British prime minister Winston Churchill could rightly say: "From Stettin [Szczecin] in the Baltic to Trieste in the Adriatic an iron curtain has descended across the Continent."

Pro-Soviet governments would stifle freedom of speech, religion, and the press and follow the Soviet Union in a faithful anti-West policy that would last for decades.

2 Everyday Life Under Communism

The Soviet system of communism promised that all would be equal—none poor, none rich. It promised to provide everyone with housing, jobs, pensions, and medical care. In *Workers' Paradise Lost* author Eugene Lyons reports that Stalin said in 1935, "For two or three years now, we no longer have any poor, unemployment has ceased, undernourishment has disappeared and we have firmly entered the path to prosperity."[15] On a basic level communism delivered on its promises. Citizens received promised housing, jobs, pensions, and health care. But the system produced these things only at the most primitive standard of performance. And commu-

A street in Russia typifies the bleak existence of its people. A car would be considered a luxury. Just finding the basics—food and clothing—was a daily struggle.

We Should Make Demands of the Party

Discontent grew not only over large theoretical issues but over day-to-day problems of a system that produced shoddy goods and a poor quality of life. In God's Playground *historian Norman Davies quoted from Polish poet Adam Wazyk's 1955* Poem for Adults, *which read in part:*

We should make demands on this earth
About overworked people,
About keys that fit locks,
About houses with windows,
About walls without mildew,
About the hatred of scraps of paper,
About people's precious, holy, time,
About the simple distinction between words and deeds.
We should make demands on this earth,
which we didn't win in a game of chance,
which cost the lives of millions,
demands for the plain, for the harvest of freedom,
for fiery, good sense,
for fiery good sense.
We should make demands daily.
We should make demands of the Party.

nism did not deliver at all on equality. The Communist Party elite enjoyed a system of privileges while most Soviets lived poorly, suffering from shortages and shoddy services and products.

Soviet workers' living standards were well below those in the United States or Western Europe. Real Soviet wages were only at the 1928 level (the last year of Lenin's New Economic Policy) in the mid-1950s. This meant that in the 1950s the average living standard of a Soviet worker was about the same as it had been in 1913, the last peacetime year under the czar. Throughout the history of the Soviet Union the quality of life lagged far behind the West. The average Eastern bloc [Eastern European communist countries] citizen could only dream of goods and services Westerners took for granted.

The good news about Soviet communism was that it provided basic security for workers. The bad news was that people understood they were guaranteed jobs and that productivity was not important. A popular Soviet wisecrack stated: "They pretend to pay us and we pretend to work."

By 1989 a number of startling facts about life in the Soviet Union had emerged. Twenty-eight percent of Soviets lived below the official poverty line—which was the equivalent of just $1,920 a year. Industries poisoned the environment with widespread pollution. Thirty million Soviets drank unsafe water. The average Russian earned 200 rubles a month (officially $320, but actually far less). While rents and food prices were set officially low, other prices put many products far beyond the reach of the common person. A pair of blue jeans cost between 200 and 400 rubles, a used foreign car between 50,000 and 150,000, a pair of sneakers between 400 and 500.

Stores, restaurants, and hotels featured terrible service. Restaurant personnel would often take their meals at exactly the time most people would want to eat and would close their restaurants to do so. "The Soviet economy is a command economy, not a demand economy. It is run for the producers, not for the consumers," summed up Hedrick Smith in *The New Russians*.[16]

There was even an inequality based on geography in the Soviet Union. Larger cities received far more food and consumer goods than did the countryside, so people flocked to them. Each day six million people descended on Moscow, snapping up 40 percent of its food and 57 percent of its consumer goods.

Thefts by workers from Soviet enterprises ran rampant. One famous joke involved a worker who leaves his factory every day, pushing a wheelbarrow with a piece of cloth over it. The security guard lifts the cloth and looks all around the wheelbarrow but finds nothing. This happens several times. Each time the guard detects nothing. Finally the frustrated guard begs the worker to please tell him what he is stealing. "Wheelbarrows," comes the answer.

Poor communications abounded. In communist Poland one manager had three phones on his desk, hoping to improve the chances that *one* of them would work. "Theoretically, you can call Germany," he said. "Well, I wish you luck, because you can never get through."[17]

Shortages, Black Markets, and Block-Long Lines

Because the system promised employment to everyone, factories and offices were overstaffed. All workers were equal, so no incentives existed for doing good work; no penalties for poor performance. Incompetent and lazy workers knew they would not be fired. Good workers knew they would not be rewarded. Few cared about producing quality, resulting in shoddy goods and services. "Even if I don't work hard at it, for my job they pay me one hundred sev-

With no main water supply in her rural village, this Soviet woman must haul water in buckets to her home. While the nation devoted its resources to maintaining military dominance, a vast number of Russia's people lived without the simplest of conveniences.

enty rubles a month," said one producer at a Moscow television station, as quoted by author Hedrick Smith. "If the show is no good—boring—they pay me one hundred seventy rubles. If I work hard and kill myself and the show is very popular, they still pay me the same measly one hundred seventy rubles. So does that make sense?"[18]

One part of the Soviet state, however, would not accept—and did not have to accept—poorly made merchandise. Military inspectors could reject products they felt were substandard. One army inspector approved only two or three of every one-hundred transistors a certain factory produced. But the average consumer did not have that luxury and lived with items that were often outright junk.

The Black Market

The system also produced chronic shortages. Poor productivity was part of the problem. Just as important, however, was the practice of controlling prices. In many cases the government set prices artificially low. The people quickly grabbed every available item. When an American supermarket offers a special on soft drinks or paper towels or ice cream, those items sell out very quickly, and the shelves become empty. Imagine that happening every day. Then imagine the companies who make those products not having any incentive to make more.

In any country, to get around such controls, large quantities of goods move into the black markets, where higher prices more realistically reflect customers' demand. In the Soviet Union the black market was huge.

In the absence of a functioning economy, a large and vital black market flourished in Russia. Here, peddlers display goods at a black market in Moscow.

Helping to fuel that black market were highly desirable goods from abroad. Foreign travel was the ultimate privilege under communism. If the Communist Party trusted that you would not defect, you could visit foreign countries. One reason such travel was popular was people could buy all sorts of goods abroad that were not available at home, and then sell them for huge profits when they returned. In the mid-1970s one ballet dancer admitted he could make about eight thousand dollars on the black market just from items smuggled back in his suitcase. With such profits to be made, he said "people would kill their own mother to go abroad."[19] Of course there was the risk of being found out by customs agents. These officials were often motivated not so much by any

Obsequiousness and Obedience Are Rewarded by Privilege

Ordinary citizens were outraged by the privileges that the Communist Party elite enjoyed. So were many members of the party, such as Czechoslovakian leader Alexander Dubcek, Mikhail Gorbachev, and Boris Yeltsin. In his autobiography, Against the Grain, *Yeltsin described the system and how it worked:*

"Obsequiousness and obedience are rewarded in turn by privilege: special hospitals, special vacation retreats, the excellent Central Committee canteen, the equally excellent service for home delivery of groceries and other goods, the Kremlin telephone system, the free transportation. The higher you climb up the professional ladder, the more comforts surround you and the harder and more painful it is to lose them. Therefore the more obedient and dependable you become. It has all been most carefully devised: A section chief does not have a personal car, but he has the right to order one from the Central Committee car pool for himself and his immediate staff. The deputy head of a department already has his personal Volga [Soviet automobile], while the head has another and better Volga, fitted with a car phone. But if you climbed all the way to the top of the establishment pyramid, then it's full communism! and it turns out that there was no need of the world revolution, maximum labor productivity, and universal harmony in order to have reached that ultimate, blissful state as prophesied by Karl Marx. It is perfectly possible to attain it in one particular country—for one particular group of people."

sense of duty but by how much *they* could get for Western goods after they had confiscated them.

Because of the shortages created by the system, Eastern bloc citizens spent a large part of their free time waiting in long lines for goods—often more than ten hours a week. People always carried string shopping bags with them so they could take advantage of whatever available goods that they might happen upon.

Recalled *New York Times* reporter Hedrick Smith in his book *The Russians*:

Personally, I have known of people who stood in line 90 minutes to buy four pineapples, three hours for a two-minute roller coaster ride, 3 and a half hours to buy three large heads of cabbage only to find the cabbages were gone as they approached the front of the line, 18 hours to sign up to purchase a rug at some later date, all through a freezing December night to register on a list for buying a car, and then waiting 18 more months for actual delivery, and terribly lucky at that.

Lines can run from a few yards to half a block to nearly a mile, and usually they move at an excruciating creep.[20]

Medical Care

Medical care, although promised free to all citizens, lagged behind the West's. The Soviet system churned out more doctors than any other nation but trained them less and paid them poorly. Medicines were in short supply. Newer drugs were not available at all. Hospitals were often so crowded that beds were placed in the corridors. Dentists relied heavily on pulling their patients' teeth. Anyone wanting decent health care would often have to resort to bribery. In exchange for better care patients would eagerly slip doctors money or presents or help out in purchas-

---

Eighteen People in an Apartment

The Soviet system never delivered on its promises of better living standards for its people. This was particularly true for housing. Yuri Krotkov defected to the West in 1967. His description of his old apartment ("better than normal by Moscow standards") appeared in Eugene Lyons's Workers' Paradise Lost:

"Our apartment contained eleven rooms. It had one kitchen with eight gas-rings, three [door] bells (one general and two individual), a telephone in the corridor which was in constant use, a bath and a lavatory, which only the fastest were able to get to in the morning (the others always stopped in the public lavatories on their way to work). There were eighteen people in the apartment, besides myself.

Seven families, seven meters for electricity, seven tables and cupboards in the kitchen, and seven launderings a month, since none of my neighbors used state laundries. This was not because they did not like them, but because they were economizing. There was not a single washing machine in the apartment; we had never even heard of a clothes-drier. But there were three television sets and two radios. Furthermore, all eighteen people ate at home. They never went to even the cheapest cafeteria, much less a restaurant. Again it was because of the expense. . . . My apartment was somewhat typical. But at the same time we were exceptional, in that each resident could say with satisfaction: 'it's crowded, but the people, thank the lord, are decent. They don't spit in their neighbor's soup, as they do in Apartment 5.'"

---

ing scarce goods. "You know," admitted one doctor, "many doctors think the best kind of patient is a sales clerk from a shop, someone who can help the doctor buy something useful."[21]

High-ranking Communist Party leaders were, or course, exempt from this system. The Ministry of Health's Fourth Department operated special clinics and hospitals for the party elite. In the late 1980s the health care system spent an average of $3,014 a person for the highest ranking sixty-nine thousand Soviet leaders compared to just $117 each for everyone else.

In 1989, 65 percent of the country's four thousand rural hospitals had no hot water; 27 percent lacked sewage systems; 30 percent had no indoor plumbing. A severe shortage of disposable needles spread diseases such as AIDS. Soviet medicine needed an estimated 100 million disposable syringes a year. Soviet industry produced only 7.8 million.

Conditions in other Eastern bloc nations mirrored those in the Soviet Union. Poland had one of the highest infant mortality rates in Europe. Communicable diseases ran rampant. In 1989 Poland had 72 cases of tuberculosis per 100,000 persons, compared to just 0.7 per 100,000 in the United States. Basic medical supplies such as aspirin, catheters, surgical gloves, and medical books were in short supply. *USA Today* quotes one Polish doctor: "We have no more than 30 percent of the drugs that should be in constant supply."[22] Doctors and nurses were among the lowest paid workers in Polish society. While the average coal miner made 250,000 zlotys a month, the average doctor earned just 150,000. Because of these conditions, from 1984 and 1989 over two thousand physicians left Poland for the West.

Housing

Soviet housing was particularly inferior and in short supply. Buildings were constructed on a massive scale and lost all sense of proportion. Construction quality was poor. One Western reporter described his Moscow apartment, which was no doubt better than average. He noted that one end of his living room ceiling was five inches higher than the other. Elevators were unreliable. Bathroom tiles usually fell loose.

In a picture reminiscent of 1930s America, a Soviet woman and her children live in a dilapidated home with no central heating, water or sewer system. Her existence was not unusual in communist Russia.

As in so many aspects of Soviet life, the problem grew worse decade by decade. In 1960, in Khrushchev's era, 121 units of housing were constructed annually for every 100,000 people. By 1985 that amount had fallen to under 72 units, or 2 million apartments built each year, a figure less than the number of couples marrying or divorcing each year (2.8 million and 950,000, couples respectively). The situation was so bad that many divorced couples were forced to remain in the same apartment because they could find no other place to live.

As late as 1989, 15 percent of all Soviets had no bathrooms, and 15 percent of those living in cities had to share bathrooms and kitchens with other families.

Censorship

Because the Communist Party saw itself as the unquestioned leader of the workers and peasants, it did not permit any criticism of itself. This ultimately led to bans on dissent, free speech, or independent thinking. Any activity that contradicted the official Communist Party line was not allowed. In Stalin's day that could mean execution or a sentence to a Siberian labor camp. After Stalin died conditions improved, but dissent was still not safe. The KGB, or secret police, still employed hundreds of thousands of agents and informers to control every aspect of life. But the executions and barbaric labor camps were phased out. Instead, the government used more subtle measures: failing to promote people, firing them from their jobs, keeping family members out of colleges, exiling people to remote cities, or committing

them to psychiatric institutions. Only the bravest people, such as Aleksandr Solzhenitsyn, Andrei Sakharov, or Sakharov's wife Yelena Bonner dared to dissent. Many, such as ballet stars Rudolf Nureyev and Mikhail Baryshnikov and cellist Mstislav Rostropovich, who had the chance escaped to the West.

Soviet newspapers, magazines, radio, movies, and television were heavily censored. News that made the Soviet system look bad rarely appeared. For example, news of a Soviet natural disaster or the crash of a Soviet airliner would almost never be printed. When the Soviet Union was forced to buy large amounts of grain from the United States in 1973, it also was not reported.

However, negative news about the United States or the West would be noted. Sometimes the details were totally made up to make the capitalist West look bad. Newspapers would also be filled with propaganda designed to build confidence in the party. Slogans such as "Long Live the Great, Unbroken Unity of the Party and the People!" were common.[23] Poems like the following might appear on the front page of a paper like *Pravda*:

> Exciting statistics of the five-year plan
> Are filled with glittering light;
> They are like branches becoming
>   green
> On a white tree trunk of a dream. . . .[24]

Some of what the Soviets left out of their newspapers they put into a widespread system of lectures. These lectures were given at factories, schools, and clubs by professional propagandists. Sometimes they provided hard information about a bad harvest or an arms agreement. Other times they would contain untruths so blatant that the authorities would not allow them to be published in the press for fear they would be seen by Western observers. Material in this category would include slanders (often anti-Semitic in nature) against dissidents such as Solzhenitsyn or Sakharov.

Foreign newspapers, magazines, and books were not allowed. Foreign radio broadcasts such as those of the Voice of America or the British Broadcasting Company (BBC) were, except for brief periods, usually jammed. Citizens were warned not to tune in to foreign stations. "Those who touch this mud which is pouring through the airwaves on alien radio beams pollute themselves and besmirch the dignity of a Soviet citizen," advised one high-ranking commentator, according to author Robert Kaiser.[25] Loss of privileges and even jail could result for those caught listening.

Food

Russia has always been an agricultural nation. Before the Bolshevik revolution areas such as the Ukraine produced large amounts of foodstuffs, but communism ended that. The collective farms removed incentives for individual farmers. The food distribution system was poor. Tons of food rotted in the fields or on railroad cars. By 1989 the Soviet Union was forced to buy $26 billion worth of food from the West.

Food prices took 59 percent of an average family's budget, compared to just 18 percent in the United States. Even so, the average Soviet family ate only 58 percent as well as an American family, often relying on heavy starches for sustenance and enjoying little variety in their diet—and just 75 percent of what the Soviet government advised as a minimum for good nutrition.

Food distribution was a major problem in Soviet Russia and the countries it controlled. In Poland, shoppers queue up in hopes of receiving food. These citizens might wait in several lines, in front of several different shops, in hopes of buying enough groceries to make a single meal.

Alcoholism

While Western nations have serious substance abuse problems, the Soviet Union's difficulties with alcohol abuse were even worse. The statistics were almost beyond belief. Almost everyone in the former Soviet Union drank—and most drank heavily. While nearly 30 percent of the U.S. population does not drink alcoholic beverages, less that 1 percent of Soviet men and only 2.4 percent of Soviet women were teetotalers. An estimated 85 percent of all Soviet workers had drinking problems. In 1987 it was calculated that ten thousand persons had died from drinking such alcohol substitutes as perfume, fuel, and even shoe polish.

Sixty-five times more Soviet deaths were from alcohol poisoning than were those reported in the world average. One-fifth of all Soviet deaths resulted from alcoholism. Families spent 15 percent of their income on alcohol, compared to just 1.8 percent in the United States.

The problem was spreading to the younger generation. A December 1983 article in *Selska Zhizn* (*Rural Life*), quoted by Robert Kaiser, noted:

> The average age of people suffering from alcoholism has fallen five to seven years in the last decade. . . . According to research on ill patients, 90 percent of them started drinking before the age of fifteen, and one-third of them before the age of ten. In most cases familiarity with alcohol begins with the cooperation of parents.[26]

Communism had created a system that robbed its people of the ability to

To cope with a bleak and hopeless existence, many Soviets turned to alcohol for solace. Here, Soviet soldiers buy alcohol from a black market peddler in Moscow.

solve their own problems and provide for their own needs. As the problems grew, the authorities pretended they did not exist and punished those who dared point them out.

Yet to most Western observers it appeared that the peoples of the Eastern bloc could not free themselves from its grasp, that the overthrow of the party could not happen. Throughout the 1950s and 1960s abortive attempts to do so seemed to prove those observers right.

3 The First Signs of Rebellion

The Soviet system lasted for three-quarters of a century. For most of that time it seemed to outsiders to be secure, nearly invulnerable. But opposition always existed, particularly among the non-Russian peoples of the Soviet Union and in the Eastern bloc satellites.

After World War II Lithuanians formed an underground army called the LFA (Lithuanian Army of Liberation) and carried on guerrilla warfare against Soviet occupation. Ukrainian nationalism has always been strong, as well. The UPA *(Ukrayinska Povstancha Armiya)* kept on struggling for independence even after the Soviets wiped out its headquarters in 1950.

The Soviet-dominated satellites were just as hostile to the Soviet Union. Moscow did its best to keep them under control. In 1949 it tied the economies of its satellites together in a union called the Council for Mutual Economic Assistance (COMECON). The original members were the Soviet Union, Bulgaria, Czechoslovakia, Hungary, Poland, and Romania. Later East Germany, Albania, Mongolia, Cuba, and Vietnam joined. In 1955 the Soviet Union reacted to the West's North Atlantic Treaty Organization (NATO) by forming its own military alliance, the Warsaw Treaty Organization, or the so-called Warsaw Pact. The Soviet Union and many of its satellites constituted the membership. Both the Warsaw Pact and COMECON were under heavy Soviet command.

One reason the Soviets took such pains was the example of Yugoslavia and its ruler, Josip Broz Tito. In 1948, Tito had broken free from Stalin's control. He insisted that each communist country could pursue its own path. There were no Soviet troops in Yugoslavia, and because Tito had seized power on his own and had the sup-

In 1948 Josip Tito had managed to break away from central Soviet control to set an independent path for Yugoslavia. His success greatly threatened the Soviets.

port of local communists, he could get away with defying Stalin. In June 1948 Stalin responded by expelling the Yugoslav Communist Party from the Communist Information Bureau, the old Comintern. It was the first breach in the Eastern bloc.

On March 5, 1953, Stalin died. A collective leadership of several top communists ruling jointly replaced him. Nikita Khrushchev soon pushed the others aside, however, and emerged as the new Soviet leader.

Opposition Spreads

While Stalin ruled, the blunt Khrushchev had served him loyally, particularly in collectivizing the peasants' farms. But in February 1956 Khrushchev denounced Stalin in a secret speech to the Twentieth Communist Party Congress. When his talk became public, many in the Eastern European satellites thought Moscow was mellowing and hoped they could break away from the Soviet influence. A series of strikes broke out in Czechoslovakia in May 1953. A month later riots rocked East Berlin. They soon spread throughout East Germany as the nation protested the harsh local regime. Soviet tanks were called in to restore order.

Similar riots occurred in the Polish city of Poznan on June 22, 1956. Police fired on the crowd, and fifty-three people died as Poles protested a 36 percent drop in real earnings from 1949 through 1955. In response, Polish communist leader Wladyslaw Gomulka, a man with a reputation for independence from Soviet influence, took power, becoming the party's general secretary in October 1956. Khrushchev at first thought Gomulka was too reform minded and independent, particularly in regard to privatizing farms. In a face-to-face meeting, Gomulka convinced Khruschev that he would loyally follow Moscow, and a "Polish road to socialism" was permitted, giving Poland more autonomy than it had previously enjoyed under Soviet influence.

Hungary formed the most dramatic challenge to Soviet rule. Hungarians had

After Stalin died in 1953, nations within the Soviet bloc took the opportunity to challenge Russian control. One of the most dramatic revolts took place in Hungary. Residents there staged an uprising in 1956.

The Voice of the Hungarian Uprising

As detailed in Reg Gadney's Cry Hungary!, *on the eve of the Russian invasion of Budapest in 1956, new, noncommunist management took over the Hungarian state radio stations and bravely announced that old practices of censorship and propagandizing were over:*

"DEAR LISTENERS! We are opening a new chapter in the history of Hungarian Radio. For many years now the radio was nothing else but an instrument for disseminating propaganda and lies. . . .

All those who have broadcast lies from this station in the past have been evicted and have nothing more to do with the Hungarian Radio. From this hour our radio is going to be entitled to carry the names of [Lajos] Kossuth and [Sándor] Petófi. The people speaking into these microphones are for the most part new men. From now on you will hear new voices speaking on old wavelengths. From now on, in the messages sent from this station you will hear the truth, as the old oath goes 'the whole truth, and nothing but the truth!'

Several former leading members of our staff as well as several correspondents of this station have been dismissed."

carefully noted Khrushchev's de-Stalinization—that is, his policy of reforms and openness—and the rioting and bloodshed in Poland. The repressive actions of Premier Mátyás Rákosi, a hard-line communist, also angered them. Rákosi resigned in July 1956, but unrest grew. On October 23, 1956, protesters, led by Budapest students, demanded a series of reforms. These included the departure of the Soviet army and the return of former premier Imre Nagy, a reformer. "We demand that general elections, by universal, secret ballot, be held throughout the country to elect a new National Assembly, with all political parties participating," read their fifth reform as quoted by Reg Gadney in *Cry Hungary! Up-*rising 1956. "We demand that the right of the workers to strike be recognized."[27]

A crowd of 100,000 protesters called for solidarity with the Polish people. Chaos resulted when police intervened. As more crowds gathered in Parliament Square, a desperate Communist Party asked Moscow for permission to appoint Nagy as premier. When it was approved, the Hungarian uprising swung into high gear. Nagy was extremely progressive, and unlike other communists, enjoyed genuine popular support. He said that Hungary would become a multiparty state and that it would leave the Warsaw Pact and become neutral. The nation was on the verge of freedom.

Thinking that nothing could stop their newfound independence, Hungarians tear down a sixty-foot-high statue of Stalin in Budapest.

Hungarians rejoiced as crowds tore down a sixty-foot-high statue of Stalin that had dominated Budapest in the postwar era. They cut the hated Soviet star out of Hungarian flags and publicly burned portraits of Stalin and Rákosi. Political prisoners were freed.

These events alarmed the Soviets, but, nonetheless, their troops began to withdraw. According to author Harry Schwartz, on October 30, 1956, the Soviets even appeared to agree to Hungarian freedom, saying that socialist nations "can build their mutual relations only on the basis of complete equality, respect of national integrity, national independence, and sovereignty and mutual non-interference in their internal affairs."[28] Their promises proved worthless; on November 2, 1956, twenty-five hundred Soviet tanks attacked Budapest.

The Hungarian people fought back bravely but had little chance of victory. The outside world admired the courage of these freedom fighters but, not wishing to trigger a third world war did nothing to help them. Wrote Peter Fryer, then a member of the British Communist Party, and as quoted by Reg Gadney:

In public buildings and private homes, in hotels and ruined shops, the people fought the invaders street by street,

step by step, inch by inch. The blazing energy of those eleven days of liberty burned itself out in one last glorious flame. Hungry, sleepless, homeless, the freedom fighters battled with pitifully feeble equipment against a crushingly superior weight of Soviet arms. From windows and from open streets, they fought with rifles, home-made grenades and Molotov cocktails against T54 tanks. The people ripped up the streets to build barricades, and at night they fought by the light of the fires that swept unchecked through block after block.[29]

But it was no use. The Hungarians were no match for the Soviets. Two hundred thousand Hungarians fled to Austria. At least two thousand others were later executed, including Nagy and commander of the army, Col. Pal Maleter. János Kádár, a communist who had once been jailed by Rákosi, replaced Nagy as premier. Now, he took the Soviets' orders. Ultimately, however, he was smart enough to lead Hungary along what was then a relatively progressive path behind the Iron Curtain, easing collectivism and relaxing some controls.

Khrushchev himself nearly lost power when the eleven-member Presidium, nervous over Eastern bloc unrest, voted to oust him in June 1957. But he took his case to the Central Committee, which kept him in command. In 1958 he was given the title of Soviet premier.

The failure of the 1956 Hungarian uprising put a lid on Eastern bloc protest for over a decade. East Germany was the most prosperous Warsaw Pact nation, but still its citizens were dissatisfied. They did not riot or protest but, instead, fled in huge numbers to the West. The four occupying powers (the Soviet Union, the United States, the United Kingdom, and France) had divided Berlin, but Germans continued to move freely between East and West Berlin. Between 1949 and 1961 three million East Germans thus escaped from communism. On some days as many as twenty thousand people left.

That lasted until August 1961 when the Soviets and East Germans sealed off noncommunist West Berlin with the Berlin Wall. The ten-foot-high wall stretched twenty-eight miles. Watchtowers and minefields made it even more dangerous. Yet East Germans still tried to escape. They jumped out of windows, tunneled under

Before German troops arrive to seal the Berlin Border in August 1961, one lucky individual makes a dash to freedom through an opening in the barbed wire.

the wall, or used whatever means they could. Over one hundred persons died trying to flee.

Quelling Dissent

In the Soviet Union hard-liners still wished to clamp down on dissent and end reforms. In 1964 they finally ousted Khrushchev, replacing him with Leonid Brezhnev and Aleksey Kosygin. Reform tendencies reappeared again, however, in 1968 in Czechoslovakia.

In the 1960s the communist system had taken its toll on Czechoslovakia. Living standards were declining, and economic hard times created a feeling of unrest. So did a new feeling of freedom on the part of the nation's intellectuals, encouraged by Khrushchev's reforms. Old guard president Antonín Novotny tried to hold the line on discontent. According to author Michel Salomon, Novotny attacked dissenters, charging, "These are class enemies, former national socialists of the right, champions of the clergy, and social democrats who once more are spreading the opinions against which the party fought after 1945."[30]

Novotny was out of touch, though, and was replaced in March 1968 by reformer Alexander Dubcek. Under Dubcek the Czech Communist Party began decentralizing authority. It gave businesses more freedom to set prices and make decisions without party interference. Freedom of expression was expanded, as Dubcek called for the "suppression of censorship in the press, radio, and TV, [and] full liberty of artistic and cultural creativity and assembly."[31]

A sentry stands guard at the Berlin wall, erected by East Germans and Soviets in 1961 to prevent East Germans from escaping to West Germany.

The Soviet Union and its Warsaw Pact allies were afraid the reforms of what came to be known as the Prague Spring would spread to their nations. They responded to that possibility by invading Czechoslovakia on August 21, 1968. TASS, the official Soviet news agency, declared, "The sister countries align themselves firmly and energetically against all threats from the outside. They will never permit anyone to remove a link from the socialist community," as quoted by Michel Salomon in *Prague Notebook: The Strangled Revolution.*[32]

Moscow announced the Brezhnev Doctrine, which said that communist regimes would never be allowed to fall. If necessary, Soviet armies would move in to maintain them.

The Soviets arrested Dubcek and flew him to Moscow. There he was beaten and then brought before Brezhnev. In 1970 Dubcek was expelled from the Communist Party. Unlike the victims of Stalin's purges, he was not killed but was given an obscure

position in the Czechoslovak forestry service. In 1977 Czech opposition reemerged under the banner of Charter 77. Playwrights Vaclav Havel and Pavel Kohut led the group, which called for increased freedom of speech and expression.

Opposition arose once more in Poland in 1970, where Wladyslaw Gomulka had ruled since 1956. At first he was a progressive force who, like Tito, allowed many peasants to own their own land. Later his government reverted to communist economic theories and faced increased economic problems. In December 1970 Gomulka ordered a 20 percent increase in food prices. In the communist system, where there were many hardships and shortages, low, subsidized food prices were something the people demanded. Poles rioted, and Gomulka ordered his troops to restore order. His troops killed three hundred protesters, and Gomulka's fellow communists—afraid of further violence if he remained—removed him from office.

During the 1968 Soviet invasion of Czechoslovakia, Czechs defied Soviet authority. Here, a man asks a Russian soldier, "Why are you doing this to us?"

In spite of every effort by the Soviets and communist East Germany, citizens continued to attempt escapes to the West. In one such try, an East German leaps from a fourth floor apartment window to escape to West Berlin. At right, East Germans seal windows that open to West Berlin.

Edward Gierek, a former coal miner from the Silesia section of Poland, replaced him. In the city of Danzig Gierek boldly met face to face with strikers. Author Neal Ascherson quotes Gierek: "I say to you: help us, help me. . . . I am only a worker like you. . . . But now, and I tell you this in all solemnity and as a Communist, the fate of our nation and the cause of Socialism are in the balance."[33] Gierek's approach impressed the strikers, who were also well aware that if unrest continued they might well be fighting Soviet tanks. The situation calmed down.

Throughout the Soviet bloc individual dissidents challenged the system. In Yugoslavia a one-time associate of Tito named Milovan Djilas became a noted critic of the communist ideology. Djilas had been vice president of his country, and many saw him as Tito's likely heir. When Djilas praised the Hungarian uprising of 1956, though, he was expelled from the Yugoslav Communist Party. He responded by writing *The New Class*, which exposed the party and the state bureaucracy as oppressive elites who benefited only themselves. Author Eugene Lyons quotes Djilas's writings:

A new class, previously unknown in history, has been formed. . . . The monopoly which the new class establishes in the name of the working class over the whole society is, primarily, a monopoly over the working class itself . . . the so-called socialist ownership is a disguise

The Prague Spring

Harry Schwartz's Prague's 200 Days *recounted the crushing of Alexander Dubcek's "socialism with a human face," Dubcek's policy of liberalization. After the Soviets marched into Czechoslovakia, Slovak writer Pavel Stevcek reminded his fellow citizens not to forget what had happened. Soon such words could not be printed, but while they could, this is what he wrote, as excerpted from Schwartz's book:*

"The times in which we are being forced to live are not the time of words, and particularly not the time of free words. Herefore, let us declare, while still we may, that we shall not forget. . . . We shall not forget that they even ordered us to wash the blood off the paving, to level the grave mounds, and to blot out signs [of resistance]. These are crimes and wrongs which are not subject to historical rehabilitation. We ought to promise, for the second time, to preserve the original meaning and significance of words for the future, in our hearts and minds, if we are not allowed to do so in writing: breach of faith, aggression, invasion, treason, the criminal killing of innocent people, etc. As you can see, we have already been forced to euphemize [politely distort] these facts, and now one must speak of entry, stay, placement, and it is only good that we need not write about a friendly visit by troops of the five Warsaw Pact countries. . . . We will certainly not be permitted to write accurately; well, at least let us read accurately."

Flag-waving Czechs shout their protests as they pass a Russian tank in the days following the 1968 Soviet invasion of Czechoslovakia.

Soviet scientist Andrei Sakharov was awarded the 1975 Nobel Prize for Peace in part for his dramatic stand against Soviet violations of the 1961 Nuclear Test Ban Treaty.

for the real ownership of the political bureaucracy.

In actuality a single group manages communism in its own interests. . . . This is a class whose power over men is the most complete known in history . . . a power which unites within itself the control of ideas, authority and ownership, a power which has become an end in itself. . . . When the new class leaves the historic scene—and this must happen—there will be less sorrow than there was for any other class before it. Smothering everything except what suited its ego, it has condemnd itself to failure and shameful ruin.[34]

Djilas received a year in prison for writing *The New Class.* In 1962, when Djilas published a memoir, *Conversations with Stalin,* Tito, increasingly more repressive, jailed him for another four years.

In the Soviet Union intellectual dissent moved very cautiously, but it began emerging in the 1950s, when censorship occasionally loosened. Vladimir Dudinstev published a novel, *Not by Bread Alone,*

which told of an inventor who was persecuted by the communist bureaucracy. Students gathered in Moscow to discuss the work, and a riot broke out. Militiamen on horseback had to be called out to restore order.

The most famous controversy of that period involved writer Boris Pasternak. His novel, *Dr. Zhivago,* was largely apolitical, but in the Soviet Union enough dissatisfaction with the system was presented to make it unpublishable in the Soviet Union. In 1957 it was smuggled out to the West, where it received the 1958 Nobel Prize for literature. Because of official censorship, Soviet citizens were not officially informed of Pasternak's winning the Nobel Prize until 1987.

Novelist Aleksandr Solzhenitsyn was a far bolder and more persistent critic than Pasternak. Solzhenitsyn had first run afoul of the system in 1945, when censors intercepted a letter in which he criticized Stalin. He was sentenced to eight years of forced labor; after Stalin's death he was considered rehabilitated, meaning that he was among those released from prison and returned to a normal life. As Khrushchev attempted to discredit Stalin, in 1962 Solzhenitsyn was allowed to publish the novel *One Day in the Life of Ivan Denisovich.* For the first time someone in the Soviet Union had realistically portrayed Stalin's slave labor camps. It created a sensation.

After 1963 the government banned Solzhenitsyn's works. Solzhenitsyn smuggled his novels *The First Circle* and *Cancer Ward* to the West, where they won the 1970 Nobel Prize "for the ethical force with which he has pursued the indispensable traditions of Russian literature."

The further publication in the West of his *August 1914* in 1971 and *The Gulag Archipelago* in 1973 increased Kremlin hostility toward Solzhenitsyn. Against his will, he was exiled and departed for the West in February 1974. He eventually settled in rural Vermont.

Poet Yevgeny Yevtushenko was less steady in his protest than Solzhenitsyn. In the 1950s and early 1960s, however, his poetry delicately dared to question those who still believed in Stalinism. His 1962 poem *Stalin's Heirs* spoke of those who dreamed of Stalinism's return and felt uncomfortable with Khrushchev's reforms. As quoted by author Roland Gaucher, the poem read, in part:

> Certain inheritors prune their rose-
>   bushes in their retreats
> And think to themselves that retire-
>   ment is only temporary.
> Others even attack Stalin from the
>   rostrum,
> But at night they yearn nostalgically

for the time that is gone:
> It is no accident that they suffer heart
>   attacks,
> They do not like the times.[35]

Yevtushenko's 1961 poem, *Babi Yar*, reminded his countrymen of the Nazis' murder of ninety-six thousand Ukrainian Jews during World War II. His 1963 memoirs *Precocious Autobiography*, however, caused Soviet authorities to turn against him. Afterwards Yevtushenko's work tended to be less controversial.

Andrei Sakharov was neither a novelist nor a poet, but a noted scientist. For his work in developing the Soviet Union's first hydrogen bomb Sakharov three times won the prestigious title Hero of Socialist Labor. But Sakharov protested the Soviets' violation of the 1961 Nuclear Test Ban Treaty. In 1968 he called for nuclear arms reduction and in 1970 founded the antigovernment Committee for Human Rights. For his courageous work in defense of civil liberties, international disarmament, and nuclear arms control he won the 1975 Nobel Prize for peace. In 1980 the Kremlin stripped Sakharov of his decorations and forced him and his wife Yelena Bonner to live in internal exile in the distant city of Gorky, away from his fellow dissidents and from Western reporters.

All these brave failures in support of freedom, nonetheless, had their value. They gave quiet inspiration to peoples throughout the Soviet bloc and helped lead, in part, to Poland's Solidarity movement—the first great explosion in the collapse of communism.

Chapter

4 Poland: Solidarity Defeated

The first great challenge to communism in Poland came not from crowds attacking tanks, but from the broadly based Solidarity trade union movement. Led by electrician Lech Walesa, Solidarity found itself on the verge of changing Poland in 1981, but that nation's government harshly cracked down on Solidarity and drove it underground. It would not remain underground forever.

Polish prime minister Edward Gierek's regime began with a new spirit of openness and change. Censorship was eased. In the first five years of Gierek's rule, Polish real wages rose by 40 percent; by 1973 Poland had the world's third highest growth rate.

Conditions, however, quickly soured. Censorship again increased. In order to favor government-owned farms, the government deprived private farms, which produced most of Poland's foodstuffs, of needed supplies and equipment. Price controls and censorship increased. Most importantly, the government made poor decisions on how to use the $23 billion dollars Poland had borrowed from abroad and launched a series of inefficient enterprises. Another big problem was the amount of money allotted to food subsidies, as the government attempted to placate public opinion by providing its basic needs as cheaply as possible.

By 1980, 40 percent of the state budget went to keep food prices artificially low. For example, farmers earned ten zlotys for producing a liter of milk that sold in the stores for four zlotys. It was cheaper to feed loaves of subsidized bread to cattle rather than feed them wheat.

Polish prime minister Edward Gierek's regime began with a new energy that eased censorship and increased living standards. The improvements, however, were short-lived.

The Beginnings of Protest

The first sign of trouble came in June 1976. The government bowed to reality and sharply hiked food prices. Strikes broke out across the country. Some thought Gierek's defense minister, Wojciech Jaruzelski, would use the army to restore order. Jaruzelski began his army career with the Polish army that had been organized in the Soviet Union during World War II, and he rose rapidly through the ranks, becoming defense minister in 1968. But Jaruzelski refused to cooperate with Gierek and is quoted by author Lawrence Wechsler as saying: "Polish soldiers will not fire on Polish workers."[36] Gierek retreated and rolled back prices.

June 1976 saw the start of organized resistance to the Polish communist system. Writer Jacek Kuron helped form the committee for the Defense of Workers' Rights (KOR). It aimed at bridging two of the main groups opposing the regime: the intellectuals and the workers. Said Kuron, as quoted by Wechsler:

We were ashamed that the intelligentsia had been silent in 1970 and 1971, and we wanted to restore its good name. After the brutal suppression of workers' strikes and demonstrations, thousands of workers all over Poland found themselves without jobs. Police stations were full. . . . KOR set itself the aim of organizing financial help for people dismissed from work

Sham Socialism

In 1979 intellectual dissent began to seep into official Polish reports. Neal Ascherson's The Polish August *told of a government commission that was formed to study the nation's problems. One participant boldly complained:*

"We are faced with sham planning and the sham implementation of plans, sham accomplishments in industry, science, the arts and education, the sham declaration and fulfillment of pledges, sham debates, sham voting and elections, sham concern for social welfare and the appearances of government, sham socialism and social work, sham freedom of choice, sham morality, modernity and progress, the opening of ostensibly completed factories and social facilities with great pomp and circumstance, the sham struggle against wrongdoing and the sham contentment of all citizens, sham freedom of conviction and sham justice. The playing of this game . . . has become so widespread that no one, not even the highest levels of government, can distinguish any longer between what is real and unreal."

The Polish independence movement was given new hope when Karol Wojtyla, archbishop of Cracow, became Pope John Paul II in 1978. The pope was an outspoken critic of communism in Poland.

occurred on October 16, 1978. Roman Catholic cardinals, meeting in Rome, elected Cardinal Karol Wojtyla, archbishop of Kraków (Cracow), as pope. Cardinal Wojtyla, the first non-Italian pope chosen since 1522, took the name John Paul II. The staunchly Catholic Poles were overjoyed that one of their own now led the world's largest religion. By restoring their pride in themselves, John Paul's election also helped give Poles renewed hope that their own nation could again be free. "When he became Pope, every Pole held his head a bit higher," said one woman, according to author Mary Craig.[38]

John Paul II

The son of a Polish army officer, John Paul II had secretly studied for the priesthood during the Nazi occupation. He became a cardinal in 1967 and was known for his work on ethics, social justice, and peace.

Even the officially atheistic Polish government had to pay respectful notice to his papal election. In June 1979 it allowed John Paul II to return home to Poland for a triumphant tour. At one stop two million persons attended. Some said that one-quarter of the entire nation had seen the pope in person. His message: Poles should remain strong. Mary Craig quotes him in *Lech Walesa and His Poland*: "The Spirit will come upon you and change the face of this land," he said. "The future of Poland will depend on how many people are mature enough to be non-conformists."[39]

On economics the pope told his audience:

and the families of the imprisoned; of offering legal and—when necessary—medical help; of fighting for freedom for the imprisoned and jobs for the sacked [fired].[37]

To avoid police infiltration, KOR limited membership to little more than thirty at any one time. In March 1977 another Polish human rights group, the Movement for the Defense of Civil and Citizens' Rights, joined KOR's struggle.

Dissent now grew rapidly. Underground publications were secretly published and flourished in Poland and included Aleksandr Solzhenitsyn's works. But a far more startling jolt to the system

The spirit of the Solidarity movement extended across borders. Here, West German Solidarity supporters greet John Paul II. He inspired members of Solidarity by encouraging them to keep their hopes alive.

Christ will never approve that man be considered, or that man consider himself, merely as a means of production. This must be remembered both by the worker and the employer. . . . Accept the whole of the spiritual legacy which goes with the name of "Poland." Do not be defeated. Do not be discouraged, and never lose your spiritual freedom.[40]

His rejection of Marxist materialism was a straightforward challenge to communist economic teachings.

Solidarity

Not long afterward, in December 1979, at Gdansk's Lenin Shipyard, workers gathered to commemorate the 1970 strikes. The government fired twenty-five workers. In response, a five-person workers' commission formed. An unemployed electrician named Lech Walesa was one of the members.

Walesa would eventually assume leadership of Poland's entire protest movement, the Solidarity (*Solidarność* in Polish) labor union. He was an unlikely leader for a national revolution. A carpenter's son, Walesa received only an elementary school and vocational education. He lived simply, his family of eight sharing a two-room apartment. For years Walesa had been the target of secret police surveillance and numerous arrests, yet such pressure failed to frighten him. He was plainspoken and physically unimpressive, yet as the tension between Solidarity and the government grew, Poland turned to him. Walesa's manner and lack of intellectual airs made him the ideal head of a workers' movement. "I am a worker and that's all I ever want to be," he once said. "It doesn't mean I have no ambition to learn, or to improve myself. But to the end of my days I shall be a working man."[41]

In July 1980 meat prices in Poland rose again. Workers went on strike across the country. The Gierek government did little to suppress this unrest. It usually granted wage increases to get the workers back on the job, but this time it did nothing as Gierek went off on vacation to the Crimea, a popular Soviet resort area. On August 6, however, authorities dismissed a dissident worker, Anna Walentynowicz, from her job as a crane operator in the Lenin Shipyard. Her firing, along with other complaints, caused sixteen thousand other workers to walk off the job on

August 14. The strikers made several demands: Anna Walentynowicz should be allowed to return to work; a monument should be erected honoring workers killed by police in 1970; workers should have the right to form an independent union. Barred from the shipyard, Walesa climbed over a wall to join his comrades and assume control of the movement. The strike soon spread to other shipyards; in just one day over fifty thousand Poles left work. Gierek cut short his vacation and returned home, but the walkout continued to spread along Poland's Baltic seacoast. The government cut off telephone connections with Gdansk to hobble the strikers' ability to communicate with each other but still failed to break the strike. By August 31 Solidarity and the government had reached an agreement. The strike would end if certain conditions were met: Solidarity would exist as an independent force; Roman Catholic masses would be broadcast on radio; censorship and political repression would ease. The creation of an independent union in a communist nation was a momentous event. The devoutly Roman Catholic Lech Walesa signed the historic document using a huge souvenir pen featuring a picture of John Paul II.

In September 1980 the Communist Party replaced Edward Gierek with Stanislaw Kania. The new government threw roadblocks in Solidarity's path, and it appeared it might not carry out the terms of the agreement signed with Walesa. In October, however, Solidarity finally registered as an independent trade union and received legal status.

Freedom filled the air. At its peak Solidarity had tremendous support among the Polish people, attracting ten million

The march of Solidarity continued in 1980 as striking workers in the Lenin shipyards in Gdansk protested unfair labor practices and poor pay.

members in a nation of just thirty-eight million persons. In the process Solidarity was transformed from a mere labor union or even a human rights organization into a unique mass movement. One member of the Warsaw branch of Solidarity described the electric atmosphere, as quoted by author Mary Craig:

> Hundreds and hundreds of people dropped in every day, with every kind of problem, not just how to set up a factory cell, but divorce problems, housing problems, drink problems. It was chaotic, but it was wonderful, the absolute spontaneity of it all, the fantastic enthusiasm. It was like a huge love affair. We all believed in the same things, we believed separately. And we were all very young. Older people supported us, but they couldn't cope with the sheer physical hard work, all hours of the day or night. Of course, we had the feeling of making history: we knew that, right from the start.[42]

How Not to Run an Economy

Poland's Edward Gierek borrowed large sums of money from the West and invested it in new industry. Gierek did not, however, do anything to change the inefficient communist system. The result, as the January 4, 1982, issue of Time *magazine noted, was disaster:*

"Gierek had the instincts of a high-rolling capitalist. His decision to borrow heavily abroad to finance an expansion of heavy industry was based on an optimistic, and naive, theory that new factories, using the best equipment and techniques, would turn out products that would be sold to cancel the debts. In all, Gierek imported about $10 billion worth of modern capital goods. Then he wasted all of it in textbook cases of how not to run an economy. For example, he put nearly $1 billion into developing and producing a light tractor designed by Massey-Ferguson and made at the gigantic new Ursus tractor facility near Warsaw. But it turned out that the company was not licensed to sell its products to the West and that, moreover, they were too expensive to be sold in the East. Besides, most Polish farm equipment did not fit the tractor. Result: production of about 500 tractors a year instead of the expected 75,000.

Gierek also made a deal with the RCA Corporation and the Corning Glass Works to build a color television factory outside Warsaw that was supposed to turn out 600,000 sets in 1981. Result: some 50,000 were produced, mainly because of bad management and a shortage of parts. Says Marshall Goldman, an economist who is associate director of Harvard's Russian Research Center: 'It was like a heart transplant in which the system rejects the foreign body. The factories simply were not working.'"

Growing Tension

The Soviet Union watched these events with great concern. In December 1980 rumors swirled that the Red Army might intervene in Poland. The Soviets were not happy but because of other considerations were not sure what to do. The Soviet Union was distracted, having invaded Afghanistan in December 1979. Soviet troops were now bogged down in a brutal war with Muslim guerrillas.

Months passed, and there was no crackdown. Still, significant events took place. In February 1981 Defense Minister

Jaruzelski became prime minister, adding greatly to his power. On May 13 a would-be assassin shot Pope John Paul II in Rome. Many felt that the Bulgarian secret police had been involved. Some suspected the Soviets should also be implicated.

The Polish people faced increased food shortages and long lines. Some believed that Jaruzelski and the Soviets had planned the shortages as a way to pressure the people, according to author Wechsler: "It's terrible to live like this," said one Gdansk cab driver. "They're starving us. They don't give us the freedom we need to save ourselves. Look what they're turning us into. Look at these lines. I'd rather fight them in battle than let them defeat us like this."[43]

A Martyred Past

Poles had often faced defeat and oppression. From 1795 to 1914 Prussia, Austria, and Russia had partitioned and repartitioned the country. During World War II Poland suffered great losses. Then communism took over the nation. Even in the glow of Solidarity's successes, most Poles expected a repetition of their nation's martyred past. Yet they carried on. Explained one Warsaw psychologist in Wechsler's history of Solidarity:

> You see, we are always preparing for the worst. There is a conviction that we should behave in such a way that if worst came to worst, at least our children will have the knowledge that we were a glimmer, that for a brief moment we lit a spark of hope. They will have that knowledge as they sit in their prison cells.[44]

The Polish government increased pressure on dissidents. In March 1981 police raided the offices of Rural Solidarity (an organization representing farmers' interests) at Bydgoszcz, beating up dozens of members. Rural Solidarity leaders Mariusz Labentowicz and Jan Rulewski were hospitalized.

Amid an atmosphere of growing tension, Solidarity held its first national congress. In October 1981 Solidarity named Walesa as its national chairman. He defeated opponents who wanted increased confrontation with the government. In Moscow the Kremlin described the gathering as "an anti-Socialist and anti-Soviet orgy" according to author Wechsler.[45]

In October 1981 Wojciech Jaruzelski assumed another leadership post: head of the Communist Party. It was the first time the positions of defense minister, prime minister, and party leader had been combined in any Marxist-Leninist country.

Although he held unprecedented official power, Jaruzelski was caught in the middle between the demands of Solidarity and the Soviets. Solidarity wanted more freedom. The Soviets increasingly pressured him to break Polish protests. Both Jaruzelski and Solidarity saw a clear threat of a Soviet invasion.

To keep the nation functioning—and to prevent Soviet intervention—talks took place between Solidarity and the government for a so-called Front of National Understanding. They broke down without an agreement being reached, and Solidarity voted to begin a national strike on December 17. But Jaruzelski had other ideas.

On the night of December 12–13, 1981, the government struck, declaring that there will be "no turning back from socialism." All the country's telephones and telex machines suddenly shut down. Throughout Poland Solidarity leaders were arrested. The ZOMO (secret police) seized Walesa in his apartment and flew him by helicopter to Warsaw. At first the ZOMO held him at a government guest house south of the capital, before transferring him to a prison. Other Solidarity leaders were also arrested, as was former premier Edward Gierek. Tanks and armored personnel carriers took up positions on the streets of Poland's cities,

Walesa at the Shipyard Gates

Gdansk shipyard electrician Lech Walesa rose from obscurity to lead the Solidarity movement in its battle with Polish authorities. Polish historian and journalist Andrej Drzycimski contributed a chapter to The Book of Lech Walesa *and described what Walesa was like in action, leading his fellow workers:*

"His authority amongst the strikers was unshakable. He often spoke at No. 2 Gate when the crowd assembled in front of it was calling for him, looking for him: 'Le-szek! Le-szek!' [Leszek is a nickname for Lech.] He spoke to the delegates of the workshops that were also on strike. In tense situations he smiled a lot. He was under strain yet relaxed. When he felt that those on both sides of the gates and those in the hall were supporting him, he would flatten his thick hair and smooth down his sweeping moustache. He would raise both arms with fists clenched, to greet the assembled crowd. When leaving, he raised both hands with fingers spread to form the letter 'V.' His improvised speeches delighted the crowds. He encouraged them to hold on, when a serious incident occurred, he grabbed the loudspeaker and sang the Polish National Anthem, and at No. 2 Gate he sometimes added to the anthem 'God who has saved Poland.'"

Lech Walesa remained the voice of Solidarity as the movement grew in strength and determination.

The Gdansk Protocol

When Poland's government recognized Solidarity, it was the first time an organization independent of the Communist Party was set up in the Soviet bloc. Neal Ascherson's The Polish August *notes, however, that the agreement would not challenge Poland's role as a Soviet satellite:*

"In view of the establishment of new, independent and self-governing trade unions the inter-factory strike committee declares that they will observe the principles laid down in the Constitution of the Polish People's Republic. The new trade unions will defend the social and material interests of the employees and do not intend to play the role of a political party. They approve of the principle that production means are social property—a principle that is a foundation of the socialist system in Poland. Recognizing that the PUWP [Polish United Workers Party, i.e., Communist Party] plays the leading role in the state and without undermining the actual system of international alliances, they seek to ensure for the working people suitable means of control, of expressing their opinions and defending their interests."

where curfews were imposed. All gatherings except for religious services were banned, as was the use of printing presses. When telephone calls were resumed they were strictly monitored. The government issued identity cards to all persons over age thirteen and forced them to carry them at all times. "As a soldier and the chief of the Polish government," Jaruzelski told the nation it was under martial law, as reported in *Time* magazine.[46] He blamed the situation on Solidarity's aggressiveness.

Some steelworkers and coal miners bravely held out. In Katowice, in southern Poland, police shot eight miners dead. Outside Katowice at the Piast mine thirteen hundred miners vowed to stay underground until Solidarity's leaders were freed. After food supplies were cut off, they finally surrendered.

The spirit of Polish independence, however, would not die. Half of Poland's three million Communist Party members resigned in protest. The entire staff of the popular magazine *Kultura* quit. Many college professors also resigned their jobs. In Warsaw's St. Stanislaw Kostka parish, Father Jerzy Popieluszko began the first of his Masses for Poland. According to author Mary Craig, he told the packed church: "Because freedom of speech has been taken away from us, let us therefore pray in silence."[47] His quiet resolve served as a rallying point for dissent—a dissent that ultimately could not be defeated.

Chapter

5 The Rise of Mikhail Gorbachev

While massive changes took place in Poland, the Soviet Union's new leader was pure status quo. The reign of Leonid Brezhnev has been called the Era of Stagnation. During the Brezhnev era no real economic progress took place. Very little was even attempted. Brezhnev was an unimaginative leader. He lacked Stalin's cruelty, but he also lacked Khrushchev's reform instincts. Corruption spread throughout the entire system. Even Brezhnev's own family was later found to have been mixed up in diamond smuggling and foreign currency exchange schemes.

As reported by authors Stephen Cohen and Katrina vanden Heuvel, one reformer said:

> Brezhnev was a leader only in the sense that he made himself acceptable to the political elite. When he came to power his motto was "stability," and that kept him in power for the next twenty years. He promised the elite and the country that everything would somehow be okay and that everyone in the elite would hold on to their posts. He changed things as little as possible. The result was greater problems, stagnation, corruption—all the crises glasnost has revealed.[48]

Andropov and Chernenko

After years of declining health, Brezhnev died of a heart attack in November 1982. KGB chief Yuri Andropov, a longtime

The regime of Soviet premier Leonid Brezhnev has been called the Era of Stagnation because of his undistinguished and unimaginative career.

member of the Soviet leadership, replaced him. He had been ambassador to Hungary during the 1956 Hungarian uprising and played a key role in suppressing it. Andropov had a reputation for honesty and intelligence, and it appeared he would someday become the party's leader. Brezhnev, however, had been nervous about having such a capable rival. In 1967 he made Andropov head of the KGB, knowing that no one from the secret police had ever ruled the party. Brezhnev was wrong, and Andropov succeeded him on his death.

It was widely believed that Andropov would not allow the stagnation of the Brezhnev years to continue. As KGB head, he had access to much information not available even to other Soviet leaders and was in a position to know just how badly his nation was doing. Determined to change things, he rooted out corruption and incompetence, firing many question-

able party leaders and bureaucrats. His approach produced a 4 percent increase in industrial production and a 10 percent jump in grain production in 1983.

As KGB chief, Andropov had crushed dissidents for Brezhnev, placing many in psychiatric hospitals. He was by no means willing to allow free speech and thought. According to Zhores Medvedev in his biography *Andropov*, a popular joke explained his style: Andropov, now the general secretary of the party, was speaking to a foreign journalist who asked if the people would follow his leadership. Andropov responded he was sure they would, "and those who don't follow me, will follow Brezhnev."[49] The meaning was clear: either follow me or end up dead like Brezhnev.

But just four months after becoming general secretary, Andropov became ill when his kidneys failed. He lived for eleven more months, but his reform program stalled as he spent his last five months in a hospital bed. He died in February 1984.

The front-runners to replace him were former Leningrad party boss Georgi Romanov, a hard-liner known as Little Stalin, and agriculture secretary Mikhail Gorbachev, a reformer and Andropov protégé. Neither candidate received a majority, and the party turned to a seventy-two-year-old Brezhnev crony named Konstantin Chernenko.

Those who voted for Chernenko saw him as an interim leader. He suffered from emphysema, a disease that makes breathing difficult, and he could barely function. A hard-liner, one of his few acts was to allow favorable recollections of Stalin to be published.

Yuri Andropov attempted to eliminate government corruption but was stopped by his untimely death in 1984.

Gorbachev quickly moved into the power vacuum as Chernenko's health failed. Gorbachev's influence grew. He traveled abroad and impressed foreign leaders. Gorbachev biographer Thomas Butson quoted British prime minister Margaret Thatcher, a staunch anticommunist: "I like Mr. Gorbachev. We can do business together."[50] The newspaper *Pravda* referred to him as the party's "second secretary." It was obvious he would be the next Soviet leader.

Mikhail Gorbachev: Father of Glasnost

Gorbachev was the youngest member of the Politburo, one of the oldest ruling bodies in the world. When he joined it in 1980 at the age of forty-nine, he was twenty-one years younger than the average age of its other members.

Gorbachev was raised on a collective farm in the Stavropol region of Russia. During World War II he had survived the area's German occupation. As a teenager Gorbachev worked summers repairing tractors. That, however, was not for him, and he enrolled at Moscow University where he studied law. By 1970 Gorbachev led the Stavropol region's Communist Party. There, he caught Andropov's eye and was thought of as a rising star. He became a member of the Central Committee of the Communist Party and in 1978 moved to Moscow, where he advised the party on agricultural issues. When Andropov replaced Brezhnev in 1982, Gorbachev served as an assistant to the former KGB chief.

Chernenko died in March 1985, and Gorbachev quickly replaced him. He in-

Mikhail Gorbachev and his wife Raisa (right) rode a wave of popularity with their message of reform and change. Gorbachev knew that dramatic changes were needed to revive the almost stagnant Soviet economy.

herited a system that seemed to be unraveling, with rapidly falling standards of production and efficiency. Alexander Yakovlev, one of Gorbachev's key aides, is quoted by author Robert Kaiser: "You must understand, it wasn't until 1985 that we learned just how bad things really were, particularly in our economic and financial affairs."[51] Gorbachev knew massive changes had to be made.

The foreign policy of U.S. president Ronald Reagan greatly complicated Gorbachev's situation. Reagan spent billions on arms, including the new Strategic Defense Initiative (Star Wars) missile defense system. Keeping up with the United States would push Gorbachev's already tottering economy over the edge.

To deal with the situation, Gorbachev announced two new policies—glasnost and perestroika—which would ultimately overturn the Soviet system. Gorbachev never meant for that to happen. A committed communist, he felt that his program would allow the system to survive. He put his ideas in strict Marxist-Leninist terms, according to author Robert Kaiser:

Lenin taught communists to base everything they do on the interest of the working people, to scrutinize deeply, to evaluate social phenomena realistically and from class positions, and to engage in a constant, creative search for the best ways to implement the ideals of communism. Today we are checking our deeds and plans against Lenin and his great ideas; we are living and working in accordance with Lenin's behests [commands].[52]

Glasnost and Perestroika

For decades the government had practiced strict censorship. Little could be said criticizing the established order. Gorbachev's glasnost, which is Russian for "openness" or "publicity," changed that, stressing freedom of speech and limiting censorship. Limits still remained, but now Soviet citizens could speak more openly about their society's problems. Many secrets of the past, particularly those of Stalin's regime and Brezhnev's Era of Stagnation, came out into the open for the first time. Banned authors such as Boris Pasternak could now be published. In 1988 *Dr. Zhivago* was finally made available to Soviet readers. The Soviet Union even stopped jamming the BBC's Russian-language broadcasts in January 1987, letting its citizens know what the outside world was thinking and saying. Author Hedrick Smith quotes Gorbachev as saying in June 1988: "In short, comrades, what we are talking about is a new role for public opinion in the country. And there is no need to fear the novel, unconventional character of some opinions."[53]

But glasnost was only a first step. Perestroika, which is Russian for "restructuring," came next. Gorbachev did not want to overthrow communism. He attempted to reform or restructure it because he knew that it could not continue the way it was. Inefficiency and corruption were too common. The Soviet Union not only could not catch up to the West, it was falling further behind.

Under perestroika some features of private enterprise would return. Prices would respond more to economic reality: If a product cost more to produce than it was being sold for, the price would have to rise. Planning would be decentralized, and local factories would have more control over decisions. And multicandidate elections would be held, although each candidate still had to be a member of the Communist Party.

The path of reform did not always follow a straight line. In February 1986, for example, Gorbachev told the French communist newspaper, *L'Humanité*, as quoted by Robert Kaiser in *Why Gorbachev Happened*, that Stalinism was "a concept made up by opponents of communism and used on a large scale to smear the Soviet Union and socialism as a whole."[54]

On a personal level Gorbachev proved to be extremely visible, acting almost like a Western-style politician. He met with workers and schoolchildren and, in May 1985, visited Leningrad. This was the first time in two-and-a-half years that a Soviet leader had visited a city outside Moscow. Before long he was traveling to Minsk and Kazakhstan, visiting France, and meeting with U.S. president Ronald Reagan at Geneva.

Gorbachev also began shaking up the Soviet leadership. His old rival Georgi Romanov was removed from the Politburo, and a reformer named Boris Yeltsin from the Ural Mountains region was named general secretary of the Moscow Communist Party committee.

Yeltsin was born in 1931 to poor parents in Sverdlovsk. He and the other five

Walking a Tightrope

Mikhail Gorbachev began the reforms of glasnost and perestroika to change the Soviet system and return to Marxist-Leninist ideals. Instead, he sped up the end of communism. In the May 11, 1992, issue of Time *magazine, Gorbachev's memoirs were excerpted. This quotation is from that excerpt:*

"We used to be hemmed in by the system we had in this country. We were repressed intellectually and forced to conform with stereotypes. . . . Everything had to be as simple and clear as ABC.

I knew that system from within. Essentially, the idea [of perestroika] was to break the backbone of the totalitarian monster. The party was intertwined with the KGB, the government and other organs of state power. Was I afraid of the KGB? No, I had no fear. If I had been afraid, I would not have been able to do anything. But I knew their power! I knew that what I am able to say today, I couldn't have said then. I had to beat them at their game.

Aleksandr Solzhenitsyn once said that following the middle course is the most difficult thing in politics. I can confirm how right he was on the basis of my own experience. There was once a political cartoon that showed me walking a tightrope and carrying two baskets, one filled with leftists and the other with rightists. The leftists are saying, 'A little bit more to the left!' and the others are shouting, 'A bit more to the right!' It's a good joke, but more important, it accurately reflects the situation I found myself in."

members of his family, along with their goat, slept on the floor of their one-room apartment. Although he earned a degree in civil engineering, he had to support himself doing manual labor. Yeltsin did not join the Communist Party until the relatively late age of thirty, but by 1976, at age forty-five, he had become general secretary of the Sverdlovsk District Central Committee.

In July 1985 Yeltsin went to Moscow to head the local communist committee. He made himself popular in the nation's capital by attacking widespread corruption and the privileges held by party leaders. He took the subway instead of riding in official limousines. He marched into stores and asked why there was no meat, fired hundreds of incompetent or corrupt local officials, and gave explosive speeches condemning the system.

While Yeltsin was making a name for himself in Moscow, Gorbachev was busy changing the face of Soviet foreign policy. In 1985 he suspended the deployment of

Mikhail Gorbachev was one of the few Soviet leaders to attempt to rally international support for his reform program. Charismatic and likable, Gorbachev charmed the West as his popularity waned in the Soviet Union.

SS-20 missiles against Western European targets, and he began a withdrawal of Soviet forces from Afghanistan in 1988. Although Gorbachev and President Reagan did not instantly get along, they later developed a better working relationship. It was not easy, considering how deeply each leader believed in his own system. Said Reagan in his autobiography:

> Looking back now, it's clear that there was a chemistry between Gorbachev and me that produced something very close to friendship. He was a tough, hard bargainer. He was a [Soviet] patriot who loved his country. We could—and did—debate from opposite sides of the ideological spectrum. But there was a chemistry that kept our conversations on a man-to-man basis, without hate or hostility.[55]

Setbacks

But there were setbacks for Gorbachev. One part of his early program was extremely unpopular: curbing the use of alcohol. The Soviet people had a higher per

Boris Yeltsin (left, with Gorbachev) became the popular leader among citizens of his own nation. He was seen as less tied to communism and more willing to initiate massive reform than his rival Gorbachev.

Gorbachev's credibility diminished when he attempted to hide the full effects of the disaster at the nuclear reactor in Chernobyl. Protests were worldwide. Here a Greenpeace worker helps set out three thousand crosses to commemorate the victims who died at Chernobyl.

capita use of hard liquor than any nation on earth. The majority of the nation's crime, serious accidents, and sexually transmitted diseases were blamed on alcohol. But when Gorbachev attempted to cut down on alcohol consumption by raising prices and limiting sales, his popularity fell.

Another incident shook Soviet citizens' confidence in Gorbachev. On April 26, 1986, at Chernobyl, eighty miles north of Kiev, in the Ukraine, a nuclear reactor exploded. Officials first tried to downplay the incident, claiming that only two persons had died and that no deadly radiation had escaped from the plant. Gorbachev himself went on television, blasting reports of a disaster as "a mountain of lies, the most virulent and malicious of lies," according to Kaiser.[56] Actually thirty-one were dead, five

hundred injured, and a huge area was contaminated by escaping radiation. An estimated several million persons were living on radiation-poisoned ground. Their risk of cancer, leukemia, and other illnesses doubled. Lesser amounts of radioactivity spread across the Soviet Union and Europe. The accident caused great concern both in and out of the Soviet Union and painfully pointed out the failure of Soviet technology and industry.

Another embarrassing, but far less serious, incident occurred in May 1987. On a whim, nineteen-year-old West German Matthias Rust flew a rented, single-engine Cessna 172 airplane through Soviet air defenses and landed in Red Square, in the heart of Moscow. The Soviet military was humiliated. As a result, Gorbachev fired both the defense minister and the commander of air defense forces. Adding insult to injury, Rust accomplished his feat on Border Guards' Day, a holiday set aside to honor the vigilance of those guarding the Soviet Union's borders from spies and foreign invaders.

Beginning in February 1988 Gorbachev faced problems of ethnic violence in Azerbaijan, near Iran, over the Armenian-populated area of Nagorno-Karabakh. Later that year a huge earthquake left fifty to seventy thousand dead in Armenia. The tragedy caused Gorbachev to cut short an important trip to the West.

As hard-liners and entrenched bureaucrats fought Gorbachev's economic reforms, the Soviet economy deteriorated even more.

Progress Continues

Despite these problems Gorbachev's reforms transformed Soviet society and charmed Western observers.

When Matthias Rust flew a rented plane through Soviet air defenses to land in Red Square, he dramatically highlighted how far the Soviet Union's control over its borders had deteriorated.

One of Gorbachev's more unpopular stands was his insistence that alcohol was destroying the Soviet people. Although Gorbachev had facts to back him up—alcoholism was indeed a rampant problem—people refused to cooperate, standing in lines to buy the ever-popular vodka.

Some Soviet leaders were removed from office for corruption. Brezhnev's son-in-law was placed on trial. Many of Stalin's victims had their reputations officially rehabilitated. Gorbachev personally invited Andrei Sakharov in 1986 to return from exile and live in Moscow. Religious freedoms were extended, and in 1988 Russian television broadcast Easter services for the first time. Later that year a church service was conducted within the Kremlin, and Gorbachev and his stylish wife Raisa attended a ceremony to mark the millennium (thousand-year anniversary) of Christianity in Russia.

The newspaper *Izvestiya*, as quoted by author Butson, wrote: "Now is a wonderful time. Everything that yesterday was said at the family table or in smoking rooms or in narrow circles is now being said openly."[57]

In May and June 1988, under tightly controlled conditions, hard-line communists dominated the first multicandidate elections held in the Soviet Union. Still, they were the freest elections held there since 1917.

Gorbachev received much credit for these changes, but the nation was ready for glasnost and perestroika. Said Gorbachev himself, according to biographer Michael Kort:

I disagree with what is sometimes said, that the way toward the renewal of

Gorbachev quickly established a rapport with United States president Ronald Reagan. Although the two held opposite political views, they were able to forge a working relationship.

If a "Big Boss" Stood in Line

Under glasnost, people began to speak out. Ogonyok *magazine published many letters from ordinary citizens. Christopher Cerf and Marina Albee's* Small Fires *contained many of these letters. This one was written by N. Nikolaeva in 1987:*

"Thousands of people are clinging to the special privileges you describe with both hands. These privileges affect one's psychology; they raise their holders' opinions of themselves and often make themselves callous, indifferent and blind.

If a 'Big Boss' stood in line to see a doctor at a regular clinic for two or three hours, and the doctor then treated him in five minutes; if he had to wait for two or three years for dentures; if he lay in a hospital hallway for awhile, and they didn't have the medication he needed; if he went on a tourist trip around the country, stood in line all the time for the toilet, and didn't get even half of what he was promised for his money; if he tried to repair his car without using connections or bribes; if he got back torn sheets from the laundry and had his brand-new sheets stolen; if his wife starts wearing the kind of boots they sell in the ordinary stores . . .*then* we could really expect some changes!"

Socialism is personally associated with the name of Gorbachev. That would be a contradiction of the truth. The forming of the new course is an expression of the fact that Soviet society and the Soviet people have gained an extensive understanding of the need for change. In other words, if there were no Gorbachev there would have been someone else. Our society is ripe for changes, and the need for changes has cleared its own road.[58]

Chapter

6 Poland: Solidarity Triumphant
Hungary: Goulash Socialism

The crackdown on Solidarity in December 1981 did not restore normalcy to Poland or improve the economy, and although Prime Minister Jaruzelski silenced the general public, he had not won its loyalty.

To weaken support for Solidarity, the government forced workers who had been

In Poland, the Soviet Union cracked down on the growing Solidarity movement, imprisoning six thousand Solidarity leaders, including Lech Walesa.

Solidarity members to sign loyalty pledges. They arrested one woman, whose mother was dying of cancer, at her mother's bedside, threatening her with prison unless she signed such a pledge. "There will not be so much as a lame dog to make your mother a cup of tea," they warned her, according to author Mary Craig.[59] They threatened another woman by saying that her children would be taken away and raised in government orphanages. Over six thousand Solidarity leaders, such as Lech Walesa and Catholic intellectual Tadeusz Mazowiecki, were imprisoned under harsh conditions. For a time Walesa was held in solitary confinement.

But the Solidarity leaders had their supporters. Many of the younger army guards quietly expressed support for their captives. One guard made a great impression on Mazowiecki. Author Mary Craig quotes the guard:

> One of his remarks remained in my memory because it reflected a bitter truth and also remained in my memory because it also revealed the core of that hellish machine that held us both enslaved. "There will always be someone to stand up for you," he said, "but who will there ever be to stand up for us?"[60]

In *Lech Walesa and His Poland,* Mary Craig quotes a joke that summed up the opposition to the government. Jaruzelski was visiting officials of the People's Republic of China and asked his fellow communists: "What is the numerical strength of your opposition?" They informed him it was about thirty-five million people—not a large percentage in China, a nation of over one billion persons. "Ah," said Jaruzelski on hearing the thirty-five million number, "about the same as us."[61] The difference, of course, was that Poland's population totaled not even thirty-eight million.

Under martial law, shortages grew and the government responded by raising prices by 400 percent. Soap was so hard to obtain that even doctors could not wash their hands properly.

Lech Walesa was released from prison in November 1982. Communist officials continued attempts to discredit him, using unproven rumors, but he remained a popular hero. In October 1983 he won the Nobel Prize for peace.

Father Jerzy Popieluszko continued his Masses for Poland at his Warsaw parish, speaking out against repression. He attracted large crowds, as well as the hatred of Poland's rulers. One high-ranking official publicly attacked him as "a manipulator of collective emotions" and "a spreader of political rabies," according to author Craig.[62]

In October 1984 Father Popieluszko was invited to celebrate mass at Bydgoszcz, a city northwest of Warsaw. The local priest had been threatened for inviting him, so Popieluszko gave no sermon. "Let us pray to be free from fear, but most of all to be free of the desire for violence or revenge," said Popieluszko.[63]

After mass three men accosted Father Popieluszko and his driver. The driver escaped by diving out of the moving car, but Popieluszko was trapped. His captors severely beat him, suffocated him in the auto's trunk, and threw his body over a dam on the Vistula River. Four state security officers were found guilty of the murder and

Covert Operations

According to a Time *article of February 24, 1992, Congressman Henry Hyde knew of U.S. covert operations in Poland and stated:*

"In Poland we did all of the things that are done in countries where you want to destabilize a communist government and strengthen resistance to that. We provided the supplies and technical assistance in terms of clandestine newspapers, broadcasting, propaganda, money, organizational help and advice. And working outward from Poland, the same kind of resistance was organized in the other communist countries of Europe."

I Am Prepared for Anything

After the crackdown on Solidarity, Father Jerzy Popieluszko emerged as a leader of those opposing the regime. The government bitterly resented his activities and eventually conspired to murder him. Grazyna Sikorska's book A Martyr for the Truth *reported that the priest knew the risks he was taking:*

"I realize that for the truth one must suffer—why should not I, a priest, add my sufferings to theirs? Because of this they bully me. There have been certain attempts, very crude ones, and no doubt they will continue. For example: at two o'clock on the morning of December 14 [1983], after I had already gone to bed, dead tired from making parcels of sweets for children in our local hospital, the doorbell rang. I didn't get up. Moments later, a crash. A brick with explosives had been hurled into the apartment, breaking two windows. Twice my car has been smeared with white paint. I've had two sham burglaries. I am under constant surveillance. On my way to Gdansk I was stopped and detained eight hours in a police station outside Warsaw. The driver was detained fifty hours. They are all very gross tactics, but there are larger matters at stake, and I am convinced that what I am doing is right. And that is why I am prepared for anything."

A memorial cross and stone mark the spot of Father Jerzy Popieluszko's murder by members of the Polish government.

received prison sentences ranging from fourteen to twenty-five years. Years later two senior police generals were charged with masterminding the crime.

The West Gets Involved

In June 1982 Pope John Paul II and President Ronald Reagan had met at the Vatican. They agreed to secretly aid Solidarity by smuggling into Poland equipment such as facsimile and mimeograph machines, transmitters, telephones, computers, shortwave radios, photocopiers, printing presses, and video cameras. Reported Carl Bernstein in a February 1992 *Time* maga-

zine article: "If something needed to be done, it was done," said former president Jimmy Carter's national security advisor Zbigniew Brzezinski. "To sustain an underground effort takes a lot in terms of supplies, networks, etc., and this is why Solidarity wasn't crushed."[64]

By 1985 in Poland an estimated four hundred underground publications with a total circulation of thirty thousand were in print. The U.S. Central Intelligence Agency (CIA) and the AFL-CIO (America's largest labor union) smuggled radio transmitters into the country to enable Solidarity activists to interrupt official radio broadcasts.

Once the Jaruzelski government promised to establish a dialogue with Soli-

Polish prime minister Jaruzelski speaks with a worker at Lenin Shipyard in 1985. As the communists lost their grip on Poland, a dialogue began between the government and the popular labor movement.

Half Open, Half Secret

After the crackdown on Solidarity, the Vatican and the United States funneled aid to the Polish underground. In the February 24, 1992, issue of Time *Wojciech Adamiechi, an organizer and editor, said:*

"Officially I didn't know the church was working with the U.S. We were told the Pope had warned the Soviets that if they entered Poland he would fly to Poland and stay with the Polish people. The church was of primary assistance. It was half open, half secret. Open as far as humanitarian aid—food, money, medicine, doctors' consultations held in churches, for instance—and secret as far as supporting political activities: distributing printing machines of all kinds, giving us a place for underground meetings, organizing special demonstrations."

darity, the United States lifted the economic sanctions it had imposed on Poland after the December 1981 crackdown. This, however, did little to lift Poland out of its difficulties. Inflation worsened, growing from 15 percent in 1985 to 17.5 percent in 1986, 25.3 percent in 1987, and 60 percent in 1988. By 1989 it soared to 650 percent. Housing was still scarce; in order to get a new apartment the average Pole waited twenty years.

In April and May 1989 new strikes broke out in the Gdansk shipyard. The government granted no concessions. With Poland's economy collapsing, Gorbachev bluntly told Jaruzelski that he could no longer rule without Solidarity's cooperation. The banned union met with the government, and on April 18 Solidarity became a legal entity again. Free elections were planned, although Solidarity members were permitted to run for only one-third of the seats in the *Sejm*, the parliament's lower house.

In June Solidarity's candidates won 161 of the 162 seats they could run for in the *Sejm*, and 99 of the 100 seats they could run for in the upper house, the Senate.

On July 14 Solidarity's influence took its place in the Polish legislature. Communists and their allies, however, still held a 299-seat majority in the 460-member body. Lech Walesa worked at prying the communists' allies, the Peasant Party and the Democratic Party, away from government control. On July 19 parliament elected Jaruzelski president—but just barely. In fact, he needed the help of seven Solidarity delegates to win. Eleven communist deputies had voted against him. On July 25 Walesa proposed to Jaruzelski that Solidarity form a new government. Jaruzelski refused and asked if Solidarity would participate in a coalition government. This time it was Walesa's turn to say no. Jaruzelski then requested Interior Minister Czeslaw Kiszczak to become prime minister and head a new government. After a few weeks of trying unsuccessfully to put together a cabinet, Kiszczak resigned as prime minister.

Meanwhile, Poland's economic crisis continued. When the government hiked food prices again, it appeared that Poles might break out into open revolt. Walesa negotiated with the noncommunist parties in parliament. "I want to help the reform wings of the Peasants' Party and the Democratic Party to get into government and answer the call of the times," he announced, according to writer Margarite Johnson in *Time* magazine.[65] Jaruzelski then asked Walesa to give him a list of three possible candidates for the prime minister's job. Walesa, known for his pragmatism, or practicality, wisely left his own name off the list. Jaruzelski chose low-key Tadeusz Mazowiecki as Poland's first noncommunist prime minister since before World War II.

Jaruzelski, however, refused to surrender. His offer had a catch: Communists would retain the key areas of police, defense, and secret service. On his first day on the job, Mazowiecki proved to be very different from his communist predecessors, foregoing his official limousine and, instead, riding his bicycle to work.

Mazowiecki instantly faced difficulties. When railway workers in Lodz, Poland's second largest city, went on strike, Lech Walesa begged them to return to work. "Mazowiecki's is an extremely difficult mission," he said, "and he has many enemies among those who do not like the political breakthrough we have achieved."[66]

The workers returned, but inflation and shortages remained, and divisions grew within Solidarity. Soon Lech Walesa was criticizing Mazowiecki. "Society is furious and fed up," warned Walesa on September 29.[67]

Walesa wanted faster changes in the

Strikers continue their protests in May 1988, two years before Poland made its final break from Soviet control.

economy, and on January 1, 1990, he got his way. The government decontrolled prices, slashed subsidies, and froze wages. The result was 60 percent inflation in January alone and another 30 percent in February: electricity, natural gas, and hot water rose 500 percent, and coal even worse; gasoline doubled in price overnight, and transportation costs nearly tripled. Experts expected real income to drop by 20 percent. By June it had actually fallen 40 percent.

On January 1, 1990, Poland officially changed its name from the People's Republic of Poland to the Republic of Poland, the country's pre–World War II name. On January 29 the Communist Party voted to dissolve itself, and in May, Solidarity candidates easily swept elections to local councils.

That summer Walesa's supporters organized a new political party—the Social Democratic Union, while his opponents in Solidarity organized the Democratic Union. Several other political parties sprang up. Rural Solidarity and the left-wing Renewal Party represented rural voters; the Confederation for Independent Poland was conservative; the Christian Democratic Party was moderate; the Socialist Party and the Social Democracy of the Polish Republic (the former communists) operated on the left.

Lech Walesa had now openly broken with Prime Minister Mazowiecki. He opposed Mazowiecki in presidential elections and eliminated him in the first round of voting. In the runoff on December 9, 1990, Walesa won a six-year term as Polish president with 75 percent of the vote. Walesa took over Poland with inflation running at 900 percent a year. The costs of such necessities as gas, central heating, and hot water continued to skyrocket. The next day he was quoted by Colleen Fitzpatrick in *USA Today:* "There are terribly difficult tasks waiting for us," warned Walesa. "I hope we will be building Poland's future together. I want to behave firmly. I want to correct everything that is wrong."[68]

Lech Walesa became more outspoken as Solidarity regained speed. In 1990, he won a six-year term as president with 75 percent of the vote.

Although Tadeusz Mazowiecki was Poland's first non-communist prime minister since before World War II, his lack of action left the door open for his defeat by Walesa in 1990.

Walesa knew what he was giving up as he continued to serve his nation. He was taking over a country in deep crisis. Before the election *USA Today* writer Peter Pritchard quoted Walesa: "Even if I win I lose. I can only lose. I am a Nobel winner. I [could] travel, go on a speaking tour, make a lot of money and come back in 10 years when the revolution is over."[69]

Hungary

After Soviet tanks restored communism to Hungary in 1956, János Kádár became general secretary of that nation's Communist Party (known officially as the Hungarian Socialist Workers' Party). At first Kádár was repressive, but eventually he mellowed and became one of Eastern Europe's more tolerant rulers. In 1962 he declared a general amnesty for political prisoners. Hungarian economic reform began in 1968 with the New Economic Mechanism (NEM), which quickly became known as "goulash socialism" after a popular Hungarian food. The NEM helped free the Hungarian economy from the drawbacks of centralized state planning. Prices were allowed to rise or fall in relation to what items actually cost to produce. Farmers were also given the power to form cooperatives in which they had some control over decision making. In 1983 a bond market opened in Budapest, the first in the Eastern bloc.

Still, even though the nation had borrowed huge sums from Western nations, Hungarian living standards lagged behind those in the West. Said expert Marshall Goldman:

> While the quality of Hungarian life and the stocks of consumer goods in the warehouses make it appear that the Hungarian standard of living is considerably more attractive than it is in the Soviet Union, by any objective standards, Hungarian economic reform [was] not a success story.[70]

Hungary was also hurt by the 1973 OPEC (Organization of Petroleum Exporting Countries) oil embargo, which increased the price of goods imported from other Eastern bloc states. Although Kádár remained in power, hard-liners regained influence in the Hungarian Socialist Workers' Party and slowed the reform process. After 1979 reformers again gained greater control, but their efforts were often frustrated by the more orthodox communists. In 1988 Karoly Grosz replaced Kádár as the party's general secretary. Kádár held the largely ceremonial post of party president until his death in July 1989.

As Kádár's power declined, various reform groups both within and outside the party had arisen. In September 1987 the Hungarian Democratic Forum was established. In its new year's 1989 issue, the progressive *Reform* magazine boldly stated that the Soviet crushing of the 1956 revolt had been wrong. Party reformers such as Minister of Culture Imre Pozsgay slowly but steadily moved toward a multiparty system.

In 1989 events accelerated. Hungarian communism was coming to an end. On May 1 officials made the nation's border with Austria the first open border between East and West. Noncommunist political

János Kádár became general secretary of Hungary's Communist Party in 1956. Kádár declared a general amnesty for political prisoners and began reforms in the Hungarian economy.

In 1988 Karoly Grosz replaced Kádár as secretary of the Communist Party in Hungary.

A Wind at Our Backs

Hungary made the transition from communist to noncommunist state in smoother fashion than any other East European country. Part of the reason was the presence of many reform-minded communists such as Minister of Culture Imre Pozsgay. In an article by Stephen Smith and Michael Meyer in the October 16, 1989, issue of Newsweek *Pozsgay is quoted:*

"What you call the East bloc is an artificial linkage, a hybrid imposed after Yalta. The crisis of Europe lies in its division. Protracted problems here will lead to protracted problems in Western Europe as well. We have an unprecedented opportunity for creating a united Europe. It's not a matter of money. We want access to western technology, to economic innovation and foreign investment. We want entrepreneurs who can teach us management skills as well.

We have seen no sign that Moscow wants to pull us back. To the contrary, Gorbachev's *perestroika* is a wind at our backs. Hungary has reached a point where there is no turning back.

The Hungary of the future will be similar to West European social democracies. The party state will cease to exist. Dictatorial socialism will disappear. We must create a constitutional state ruled by law. The goal should be a parliamentary government freely elected from among competing parties. If defeated, the party will transfer power as in any democracy. Hungary is not an oligarchy; we should be able to change our leaders at any time."

Reformer Imre Pozsgay led the movement to end communism in Hungary.

A Hungarian soldier tears down part of the historic Iron Curtain border fortification as communism in Hungary faded into history.

parties formed the Opposition Round Table to negotiate an end to communist one-party rule. According to *Newsweek* writer Michael Meyer, Imre Pozsgay had said in October:

> Communism does not work. We must start again at zero. . . . It's time the dictatorship of the proletariat disappears. Now we must create a constitutional state. . . . We have always been like a ferry boat, plying the river between East and West. For too long we have been moored to the Eastern bank. Perhaps soon we will have a berth on the Western shore.[71]

On October 11, 1989, 1,274 delegates of the Hungarian Socialist Workers' Party formally abandoned communism and overwhelmingly voted to change their name to the Hungarian Socialist Party. The communist symbol of the red star was removed from all official buildings, and General Secretary and Premier Karoly Grosz was sent packing. On October 19 the National Assembly voted to allow political parties. The National Assembly dissolved itself and scheduled free elections for March 25, 1990.

Poland and Hungary had led the way toward East European freedom.

7 The Rest of the Bloc Breaks Away

As Poland and Hungary broke away from communism and Soviet domination in 1989, popular discontent caused governments to fall from East Germany in the north to Bulgaria in the south.

Ten Years for a Trabant

East Germany appeared to be the economic success story of the Eastern bloc. When economic progress in other COMECON nations ground to a halt, the East Germans reported gains. Part of this stemmed from the traditional German work ethic and efficiency. However, the East Germans also benefited from over one billion dollars in annual subsidies from West Germany and from access to the European Common Market through West Germany.

Yet East Germany prospered only by contrast to its impoverished Marxist-Leninist neighbors. Compared to its more prosperous West German cousin, East Germany was an economic embarrassment. East German workers made only one-third as much as West German workers. Their industries turned out less reliable goods. For example, while West Germany produced such popular and dependable cars as the

Volkswagen, the Audi, and the Mercedes-Benz, the East Germans came out with the Trabant in 1957. Conceived as an Eastern bloc version of the Volkswagen, the Trabant's design never changed. Poorly designed, with a plastic body and a two-stroke engine, the Trabant was no one's dream auto. The Trabant cost the average East German the equivalent of a year's wages, and there was a ten-year waiting list to obtain one.

If not for the Berlin Wall, hundreds of thousands, perhaps millions, of Germans might have fled to the West. The wall symbolized communist oppression. President John F. Kennedy had spoken out against it when it was built in 1961, and it continued to cause friction in international affairs. In June 1987 President Ronald Reagan boldly issued a challenge to Mikhail Gorbachev to "tear down this wall!"[72]

At the time, it seemed unlikely this would happen. The following year East German Communist Party general secretary Eric Honecker predicted the wall would last a century. But, as the winds of change swept Eastern Europe, East Germany would not be left behind.

When Hungary opened its border to noncommunist Austria in 1989, East Germans swarmed through Czechoslovakia to Hungary and then escaped to the West. In

Mr. Gorbachev, Tear Down This Wall!

The Berlin Wall was a visible symbol of communist oppression. Few believed it possible that it would be torn down in the near future. In June 1987, however, President Ronald Reagan visited West Berlin and issued this challenge to Mikhail Gorbachev, as quoted in his autobiography An American Life:

"From the Baltic, south, those barriers cut across Germany in a gash of barbed wire, concrete, dog runs, and guard towers. Farther south, there may be no visible, no obvious, wall. But there remain armed guards and checkpoints all the same—still a restriction on the right to travel, still an instrument to impose upon ordinary men and women the will of a totalitarian state. Yet it is here in Berlin where the wall emerges most clearly; here, cutting across your city, where the news photo and the television screen have imprinted this brutal division of a continent upon the mind of the world. Standing before the Brandenburg Gate, every man is a German, separated from his fellow man. Every man is a Berliner forced to look upon a scar. . . .

General Secretary Gorbachev, if you seek peace, if you seek prosperity for the Soviet Union and Eastern Europe, if you seek liberalization: Come here to this gate! Mr. Gorbachev, open this gate! Mr. Gorbachev, tear down this wall!"

The Berlin Wall, the most enduring reminder of the split between East and West, is no more.

East German Communist Party general secretary Eric Honecker predicted that the Berlin Wall would last another century, proving once again that many communist leaders did not realize the inevitability of freedom.

less than a month 50,000 East Germans fled. Within a year 500,000 had left their homeland.

In early October, to prevent any further escapes through Hungary, East Germany closed its border with Czechoslovakia, but it could not keep the lid on much longer. Shortly thereafter Mikhail Gorbachev arrived in East Germany to commemorate the fortieth anniversary of the founding of the German Democratic Republic. Large crowds of East Germans begged him for help. He avoided publicly criticizing Honecker but, according to author Robert Kaiser, privately told him: "Life itself punishes those who delay."[73] Gorbachev allowed this statement to become known to reporters who then published it. Some reports also stated that he warned Honecker that Soviet troops would not help him keep control.

Five thousand young East Germans had gathered outside the Palace of the Republic in East Berlin hoping to see Gorbachev. When he failed to appear, they left and marched through the city streets shouting, "Gorby, Gorby." The East German police attacked the crowd, hitting them with riot batons and beating them with their fists.

Opposition was not just confined to those crowds. The New Forum, a group led in large part by the country's Lutheran ministers, spearheaded East German opposition. All through 1989 attendance grew at its Monday evening protests in Leipzig. The day after Gorbachev left for home, the crowd reached 50,000, the largest in East German history. Honecker ordered the use of force to smash this opposition. No one obeyed. When the crowd grew to 150,000 at the next meeting, Honecker resigned from all party and governmental positions. His replacement, Egon Krenz, was no wild-eyed reformer. Instead, Krenz was a loyal Honecker protégé, known as the aged leader's "teacher's pet."

Krenz, however, talked of reforming the system. As reported by Russell Watson in *Newsweek*, Krenz met with workers, who were surprisingly open with him. "People are fed up," said one. Another told Krenz:

East Germans and West Germans join hands to dance on the Berlin Wall and celebrate its destruction.

"We're being so open with you so that you people up there will know what's wrong." Krenz, who had long been insulated from the everyday problems of the people, looked puzzled. "What do you mean, 'you people up there'?" he asked.[74]

Krenz quickly grasped the problem. On November 8 he fired the entire cabinet. "We want a socialism that is economically effective, . . ." he had stated in October, "and most of all, has its face turned to the people."[75]

On November 9 Krenz ordered the wall opened. On both its east and west sides huge crowds gathered. As the wall was opened, people surged through from the east. Guards on the West Berlin side, at Checkpoint Charlie, did not know what to do. At first they refused to let the freedom seekers into West Berlin. They phoned their superiors for guidance as the crowds around them chanted, "Come over! Come over!" to the East Berliners. The East Berliners shouted back "We are trying," and pressed closer to the barrier.

Not waiting for the officials, a German takes a sledgehammer to the Berlin Wall to take matters into his own hands.

Protestors in Wenceslaus Square reach for pamphlets demanding freedom and honest elections.

Finally at 11:17 P.M. an American border guard, with a shrug of his shoulders, allowed the gate to swing open. Thousands of East Germans surged through. "I just can't believe it!," said thirty-four-year-old Angelike Wache, the first person across, "I don't feel like I'm in prison anymore!"[76]

The communist regime was rapidly crumbling. In January 1990 Honecker was arrested on charges of corruption, misrule, and treason. (In January 1993 a German court ruled he was too ill to stand trial and he flew to exile in Chile.) On March 18, 1990, East Germans voted the communists out of office; in September the GDR became the first member to leave the Warsaw Pact. All 370,000 Soviet troops were to be withdrawn from East Germany by December 31, 1994.

The Velvet Revolution

Since the crushing of the Prague Spring in 1968, Czechoslovakia had been a model Soviet satellite. True, some opposition centered around the Charter 77 organization and the figure of dissident playwright Vaclav Havel. But by and large Czechoslovakia was calm. All that changed in 1989.

On January 15 five thousand demonstrators gathered in Prague's Wenceslaus Square to mark the death of Jan Paluch, who twenty years earlier had set himself on fire to protest the Soviet invasion. Police used water cannons and clubs to break up the gathering.

Protests grew throughout the year. On November 17, 25,000 students marched through Prague demanding freedom and honest elections. Premier Milos Jakes responded by sending in riot police who savagely beat the marchers. Protests multiplied. Three days later 200,000 people crowded into the square. A later rally attracted 300,000, who shouted "Jakes, your time is up."

On November 24 former Czech leader Alexander Dubcek emerged from nearly two decades of obscurity. Addressing a huge crowd at Wenceslaus Square, he called for the overthrow of the government. Less than twelve hours later Jakes and the entire Czech Politburo resigned.

On December 29, 1989, Vaclav Havel won election as the first noncommunist Czech president in forty-one years. He appealed for Western understanding—and respect. "The West can help most by lending its moral support," said Havel, as quoted by Michael Meyer in a January 1, 1990, *Newsweek* article. "Do not view Czechoslovakia as a poor and limping relative who has to be helped to cross the street."[77] In February 1990 Havel and Gorbachev agreed that Soviet troops (73,500 soldiers and their families, 1,220 tanks, 2,505 armored vehicles, 77 combat aircraft, and 146 helicopters) would leave Czechoslovakia by July 1991.

The Genius of the Carpathians

In the West, Romania had a reputation as one of the more independent of all Warsaw Pact nations. In foreign policy matters this was true. Romania refused to break relations with Israel after the Soviet Union did. It condemned the crushing of Alexander Dubcek's reforms in Czechoslovakia. The country refused to allow Soviet troops to be stationed on its territory. Romanian athletes broke the Soviet boycott of the 1984 Los Angeles Olympics.

Protestors fill Prague's Wenceslaus Square in 1989 to mark the death of martyr Jan Paluch. Such protests would increase in frequency throughout the year.

Nicolae Ceausescu gave new meaning to the words repressive and cruel. His sixty-thousand-member secret police ensured the brutal dictator's complete control over Romanian citizens.

Domestically, however, Romania was not only an orthodox communist state, it was one of the Eastern bloc's more repressive members. In 1965 Nicolae Ceausescu became secretary-general of the Romanian Communist Party. As the years passed, his repression and his egotism worsened. He insisted on being known by such titles as Genius, Prince Charming, the Genius of the Carpathians, God, and Oak Tree. Such was his ego that Romanian television color broadcasting was reserved solely for coverage of Ceausescu and his wife Elena. Everyone else was shown in black and white. Because of Ceausescu's sixty-thousand-person strong secret police (the Securitate),

no meaningful organized opposition ever arose in Romania. Suspected dissidents were kept under surveillance or harassed. Fear was widespread.

By 1981 Romania's foreign debt reached eleven billion dollars. This alarmed Ceausescu, who responded with a brutal program of belt-tightening designed to quickly pay off Romania's obligations. Schools, libraries, and museums were closed. He rationed heat for apartments, offices, rest homes, and hospitals. Street lights were turned off. It became illegal to drive a private car in Romania. Almost everything of value—including large quantities of the country's meat and vegetables—were exported in an attempt to raise foreign currencies.

Ceausescu also pursued a brutal policy of forced collectivization. The government destroyed thousands of small villages, forcing residents to move into communal housing. Ceausescu, however, did not believe in such accommodations for himself or his family. They lived in a number of lavish homes including a 150-room villa in central Bucharest that featured gold fixtures in the bathrooms.

Ceausescu also began work on an $800 million structure, the House of the Republic, in Bucharest, Romania's capital. Thirty thousand laborers, including fifteen thousand soldiers, worked for five years on the enormous building.

Ceausescu vowed he would hold the line against the wave of reform sweeping Eastern Europe, but Romanian resentment broke out into the open on December 16, 1989. In the city of Timisoara in the Carpathian Mountains, thousands protested the government's transfer of a parish priest. When Ceausescu's ministers showed reluctance to break up the gathering, he threatened them with the firing squad. At least a thousand people died when troops fired on the crowd. The disturbances spread to other Romanian cities.

On December 21, 1989, the Ceausescus organized a massive progovernment rally in Bucharest. However, instead of supporting the regime, the crowd turned on their rulers. They shouted "Down with Ceausescu!" and "Yesterday Timisoara, today Bucharest!"[78] Ceausescu retreated into the building and ordered his troops to fire on the crowd. They refused, and Ceausescu realized what that meant. He and his wife fled the city by helicopter.

The National Salvation Front under the leadership of Ion Iliescu, a former member of the Communist Party's Central Committee, took control of the government. The National Salvation Front promised to bring democracy to Romania and to hold elections the following April.

Two days after fleeing Bucharest, Nicolae and Elena Ceausescu were arrested, and on Christmas Day 1989, they were secretly placed on trial and executed. "We applied the existing law, which included an emergency procedure," said a spokesman for the National Salvation Front, as quoted in the 1990 *Current Biography Yearbook*. "It was the people who demanded his death."[79]

The Prussia of the Balkans

Old-line Stalinist Todor Zhivkov ruled Bulgaria for thirty-five years and was known as Moscow's most loyal ally. He would do anything Moscow wanted. His secret police were often involved in provocative incidents abroad, such as the 1978 London murder of Bulgarian defector Georgi Markov (by use of a poison-tipped umbrella), and they were implicated in the plot on the life of Pope John Paul II.

Zhivkov was known for his strict repression. To punish opponents, he instituted brutal prison camps at Lovech and Skravena, where 147 persons were allegedly killed between 1959 and 1962. He also pursued harsh policies toward Bulgaria's Turkish minority, which makes up about 10 percent of the population. To destroy their sense of identity, he even forced the Turks to adopt Bulgarian names. Some 320,000 Turks fled the country.

The Masks Will Fall

Playwright and human rights activist Vaclav Havel paid dearly for his opposition to the Czechoslovak communist regime. His plays were banned and he was imprisoned three times. In October 1989, he could see that the old order was changing and that Czechoslovakia was entering a period of great uncertainty. Those in power, observed Havel, were about to make changes that were previously unthinkable. In the October 16, 1989, issue of Newsweek *magazine, Havel was quoted as saying:*

"A dictatorship in crisis makes contradictory moves. I can imagine a situation that one day my play will open in Prague, and the next day I'll be in prison. This may seem implausible, but at the moment of crisis, when power is shaken, anything can happen. For 20 years, the communists exploited the future. Now come the results of this very dangerous policy, [we] will be like Poland—$40 billion in debt and no basic foodstuffs. We keep telling the regime that it is not necessary to wait until the bitter end before starting a social dialogue. A lot of suffering could be prevented.

But do not forget, in a totalitarian system we can observe an interesting phenomenon. People in power will speak out only when the time is ripe. Our leaders all wear a uniform mask and declare identical phrases. Perhaps at a moment of history, the masks will fall, and it is only at that moment that we know who is who. It is possible then that we may be surprised to find that the masks concealed an intelligent face."

Try as they might, communists could not silence Vaclav Havel, who continued his outspoken campaign against communism at great personal cost.

Because of its harsh atmosphere, Bulgaria was sometimes known as the Prussia of the Balkans, a reference to the old German kingdom known for its militarism and efficiency. But even in Bulgaria unrest stirred. Zhelyu Zhelev, an intellectual who had been jailed for his writings, was quoted in a December 1989 *Newsweek* article: "It's too late to turn the clock back. If they tried, there would only be more demonstrations and rallies. There are no alternatives to democracy."[80]

Zhivkov was overthrown in November 1989 and placed under house arrest. A year later prosecutors indicted him for abuse of power and misappropriation of $3.7 million in government funds. In September 1992 a court found Zhivkov guilty of embezzling $24 million. He was sentenced to seven years in prison. Prosecutors also planned to place him on trial for his treatment of Bulgaria's Turks.

In January 1990 Bulgaria's national assembly changed the country's constitution, removing the Communist Party's monopoly on power, and approving an amnesty for more than nine thousand prisoners. The Communist Party renamed itself the Socialist Party and promised greater freedom for Bulgarians. With heavy support from rural areas, its candidates won elections held in June 1990. In October 1991 it was replaced by a noncommunist coalition government.

Yugoslavia

While Marshal Tito lived he held together the multiethnic state of Yugoslavia. The nationalities were varied: Serbs, Croats, Slovenes, Bosnians, Montenegrans, Albanians, and Macedonians. So were the religions: The Serbs, Montenegrans, and most of the Macedonians were Eastern Orthodox, the religion of most Russians, Bulgarians, and Ukrainians; the Croats and Slovenes were Catholics, who paid allegiance to the pope. The two branches of Christianity, though not very different in terms of

Upon the death of Marshal Tito, the multiethnic nation of Yugoslavia could no longer operate in unity as widespread ethnic violence and turmoil took control of the nation. (Left) Serbian nationalists demonstrate in Yugoslavia.

A Yugoslavian refugee stands before her ruined home.

doctrine, had split nearly a thousand years ago. The Albanians and many of the Bosnians were Muslims, a legacy of centuries of Turkish occupation.

After Tito died in 1980, the two million Albanians living in the nation's Kosovo region began agitating for their own republic within the Yugoslav federation when Slobodan Milosevic, the leader of the Serb Communist Party, harshly put down their protests. His brutality inspired other non-Serbian nationalities to opt for independence. They saw what Milosevic was doing to the Albanians and determined to get as far away from his power as possible. Said Dennison Rusinow, a foreign affairs expert: "Kosovo provided the fuse and Milosevic provided the detonator that has now led to explosions across the whole country."[81]

On January 22, 1990, the Yugoslav Communist Party voted to end its monopoly on state power. Under Milosevic, however, former communists remained in power in Serbia. On April 16, 1990, a relatively conservative coalition in Slovenia won the first multiparty elections held in Yugoslavia in forty-five years. Croatia and Slovenia declared their independence on June 25, 1991. The Macedonian parliament voted for independence that same month, and in September of that year 75 percent of Macedonians voted to secede from Yugoslavia. Bosnia became independent in March 1992. Fighting broke out almost immediately between the Serbs and the breakaway Croatians, Slovenes, and Bosnians.

Chapter

8 The Collapse of the Soviet Union

While the East European nations were breaking free of Soviet control, inside the Soviet Union Gorbachev faced growing obstacles. Differences between reformers and hard-liners grew. The ethnic peoples of the Soviet Union increasingly desired independence from Moscow.

The economy worsened: The gross national product dropped 10 percent in the first ten months of 1991, while prices rose 48 percent. Nutrition was poor; in 1991 only an estimated 8.5 percent of all Soviet children in grades one through ten had reached normal height and weight for their age.

Yet Gorbachev failed to make such necessary changes as closing wasteful industries or cutting military spending. From 1990 to 1991 the defense portion of his budget actually rose from 26 percent to 36 percent.

Armenians and Azerbaijanis still battled over the region of Nagorno-Karabakh. The Baltic states—Latvia, Lithuania, and Estonia—grew more restive. Lithuania was particularly troublesome for Gorbachev. In 1988 *Sajudis* (the Lithuanian Reform Party) began its struggle to restore Lithuanian culture and freedom. In December 1989 the Lithuanian Communist Party split

Empty shelves in a Moscow food store in 1990 illustrate the deep economic problems that nation faced.

from the Soviet party, and Lithuania became the first republic of the Soviet Union to permit multiparty elections. When *Sajudis* won the elections and declared Lithuanian independence, Soviet hard-liners were displeased. In January 1991 units of the KGB called the Black Berets attacked Lithuanian civilians, killing several. Similar deaths occurred in Latvia.

Gorbachev's critics blamed him for not preventing the violence and for backpedaling on reforms. Many progressives such as Alexander Yakovlev and Foreign Minister Eduard Shevardnadze resigned, warning of a "looming dictatorship."[82]

The Fall and Rise of Boris Yeltsin

Reformers no longer looked to Gorbachev for leadership, but turned instead to Boris Yeltsin. In 1987, after a fiery Politburo speech criticizing the entire Soviet system, Yeltsin was ousted as a Politburo member and Moscow Communist Party leader. In

The Coup Was Going to Happen

In 1991 many reformers, including Foreign Minister Eduard Shevardnadze, left the Gorbachev government. As Shevardnadze left, he warned Gorbachev that his hard-line enemies were plotting against him. In an interview in the October 5, 1992, issue of Time, *he reflected on these events:*

"If the coup had succeeded, the Soviet Union would have survived with all its ideological and repressive structures. Remember, I did warn that the coup was going to happen. If they had taken the necessary steps then, there would have been no conspiracy; the democratic process would have continued. The Soviet Union would have disintegrated but at a different stage, and the transition period would have been less painful.

When I say I warned [Gorbachev], that does not mean that I told him everything. I did not see everything. But what I did tell him he sometimes ignored. His vision was different. He had his own way of analyzing things. For example, when I told him that there was the danger of dictatorship, he did not take it seriously at all.

I think Gorbachev still believes in the socialist idea, the way I believed in it. He believed ideal socialism was possible. If he had been a scholar and believed that, there would have been nothing bad about it. Someone would have read his treatises, and that would have been that. But if you lead a country, your vision is very important."

1989 he bounced back, winning, with 89 percent of the vote, a seat from Moscow in the new Congress of People's Deputies. In July 1990 Yeltsin left the Communist Party altogether, saying he could no longer obey its dictates. "I have to obey the will of the people," the July 13, 1990, issue of *USA Today* quotes him as saying.[83] He increasingly attacked the pace of reforms and called on Gorbachev to resign.

Hammering away at the special privileges enjoyed by the party elite, Yeltsin vowed in his 1990 autobiography:

> As long as no one can build or buy his own dacha [country cottage], as long as we continue to live in such relative poverty, I refuse to eat caviar followed by sturgeon; I will not race through the streets in a car that can ignore traffic lights. I cannot swallow excellent imported medicines, knowing that my neighbor's wife can't get an aspirin for her child. Because to do so is shameful.[84]

On June 12, 1991, Yeltsin finally achieved a power base from which to challenge Gorbachev and the entire Soviet power structure. With 60 percent of all votes cast, he captured the presidency of the republic of Russia. Unlike Gorbachev, who had never won a direct election, Yeltsin now had a popular mandate. In July Yeltsin ordered a halt to Communist Party interference in factories, offices, the army, and even the KGB within Russia.

The Coup Begins

Although Yeltsin now ruled the Russian Soviet Federated Socialist Republic, Gorbachev still held the presidency of the

A demonstrator in Lithuania calls for freedom from Soviet rule. As the Soviet Union lost control, its satellites began to challenge and hasten its demise.

entire Soviet Union. The old guard began mobilizing. Prime Minister Valentin Pavlov sought authority to issue decrees not only without Gorbachev's approval, but without even his knowledge. In July the old-line communists issued an appeal, asking "those who recognize the terrible plight into which our country has fallen" to support harsh action to restore order.[85] It was a thinly veiled plea for a communist coup.

On Tuesday, August 20, 1991, Gorbachev, Yeltsin, and the president of Kazakhstan were to sign a treaty shifting authority over such key items as taxes and police to the various republics. The agreement also called for a directly elected Soviet president. Gorbachev hoped other republics would also sign, although Latvia, Lithuania, Estonia, Moldavia, Georgia, and Armenia seemed too far down the road toward outright independence to be interested. In any case this treaty would make restoring Soviet authoritarianism much more difficult. Hard-liners knew it had to be stopped. Time was running out for them, and they conspired to overthrow Gorbachev and halt the reform process for good.

Gorbachev seemed blissfully unaware of any danger. Even though American president George Bush personally warned him, he did not believe that his advisors had the courage to stage a coup. Gorbachev's lack of caution raised questions about his involvement in the plot.

Gorbachev also made it easier for the coup plotters by leaving Moscow for a vacation in the Crimea. The coup began at 4:50 on Sunday afternoon, August 18, 1991; when Gorbachev picked up his phone, it was dead. "I picked up a second, a third," he said, "I picked up a fourth telephone. None of them [worked]. I picked up the internal phone. Everything was cut off."[86] Then a delegation led by his chief of staff, Valery Boldin, entered the room. The group told Gorbachev he must either declare a state of emergency or resign in favor of Vice President Gennady Yanayev. Gorbachev refused. The plotters held Gorbachev captive, but security was so lax he was able to rig up a radio and listen to foreign stations reporting the coup. From the broadcasts he learned that his enemies were claiming he was too ill to remain as leader. "How could these people talk about bad health? Their own hands were shaking the whole time," he later commented, according to an August 23, 1991, report in *USA Today*.[87]

Gorbachev even found a video camera and made four separate tapes of himself, denying that he was in ill health. These he hid on the property, so that the world could later know the truth if necessary.

Boris Yelstin addresses an enormous crowd protesting the removal of Mikhail Gorbachev. The people refused to accept the government's appointment of Gennady Yanayev as president.

Demonstrations and Strikes Are Not Allowed

After arresting Mikhail Gorbachev in August 1991, the coup plotters attempted to cement their hold over the rest of the country. They put out a proclamation to the Soviet people, telling what would and would not be allowed. USA Today *printed much of their decree in the August 20, 1991, edition:*

"The committee resolves:

1. Bodies of authority and administration . . . should ensure unfailing compliance with emergency regulations.
2. To immediately dismantle the structures of power, administration and militarized units acting contrary to the constitution and laws of the Soviet Union.
3. To regard the laws and decisions by bodies of power and administration that run counter to the constitution and laws of the Soviet Union as being henceforth invalid.
4. To suspend the activities of political parties, social organizations and mass movements.
5. The Soviet Security Committee . . . is suspended.
6. Citizens . . . should hand in . . . firearms, munitions, explosives, military hardware and equipment. . . . The Interior Ministry, the KGB and the Defense Ministry . . . should secure strict compliance with this demand.
7. The Prosecutor's Office, the Interior Ministry, the KGB and the Defense Ministry should . . .

    (a) Ensure protection of public order. . . . Rallies, street marches, demonstrations and strikes are not allowed.

    (b) Resolutely curb the dissemination of instigatory rumors and actions provoking violations of law and order.
8. To establish control over the mass media.
9. Bodies of authority and administration and heads of organizations and enterprises should take measures to:

    (a) Restore order and discipline.

    (b) Ensure the normal functioning of enterprises.

    (c) Wage a decisive struggle against . . . corruption, theft, profiteering, goods concealment, bungled management.
10. To consider regular work . . . incompatible with moonlighting in entrepreneurial capacity.
11. Extraordinary measures should be taken to organize the procurement, storage and processing of farm produce.
12. Cabinet of Ministers is hereby instructed to work out, within a week, a resolution to ensure the provision . . . of plots of land for fruit and vegetable-growing.
13. Cabinet of Ministers should [draw up plans] to pull the country's fuel and power complex out of the crisis."

The coup plotters announced that Yanayev had replaced Gorbachev. On Monday, August 19, Yanayev, who had earlier said he was "a Communist to the depths of my soul," claimed that Gorbachev was being replaced for "health reasons" and an "inability to perform his duties."[88] Yanayev pledged that the coup was "in no way mean renunciation of the course towards profound reforms in all spheres of life."[89] Few Soviet citizens believed him.

The old guard was used to having the Soviet people obey their every order. They expected no real resistance and took few precautions, but they were wrong. Things

As Soviet tanks attempt to enter Red Square to repress protests, Soviet citizens block them—an act that would have been unthinkable even a few years before.

had changed so much that when Yanayev made his absurd statement, Soviet reporters laughed at him.

The plotters banned protests and strikes, announced a curfew, and restricted the media. They sent hundreds of tanks into Moscow but, unlike Poland's Wojciech Jaruzelski, made no effort to close the airports or to control radio, television, and telephones. Resistance flared up instantly.

Yeltsin on a Tank, Flowers in Gun Barrels

Boris Yeltsin quickly emerged as the leader of the opposition and demanded that the plotters release his old rival Gorbachev. He climbed on top of a tank outside the home of the Russian parliament, often called the "White House," and told two hundred supporters, "The actions are illegal," according to the August 20, 1991, issue of *USA Today*.[90] His courage rallied resistance. Soon tens of thousands of persons joined the crowd, serving as a shield for the White House and for those reformers inside.

Yeltsin placed thirty tanks outside the parliament to protect it. Inside, deputies and their supporters handed out guns and were ready to fight if tanks stormed the building. Later Yeltsin spoke to the Soviet citizens and gave interviews to foreign journalists. The outside world looked on the coup with alarm. From London to Tokyo stock markets dropped.

The next day—Tuesday, August 20—the plotters sent one hundred tanks to seize the White House, but hundreds of thousands of Moscow residents gathered

Although Soviet communists tried to head off the collapse of the nation, it was inevitable. Here citizens in the Baltics declare their independence.

around the building, surrounding the tanks and soldiers. Some protesters stuffed rosebuds and wildflowers into the gun barrels of soldiers. Others tossed Molotov cocktails [crude bombs made of bottles filled with flammable liquid] at the tanks. When they surrounded one tank six hundred yards from the parliament, the soldiers inside opened fire and killed four people. Some tank drivers and paratroopers defected to the opposition.

Yeltsin, Gorbachev's foreign minister Eduard Shevardnadze, Yelena Bonner (Andrei Sakharov's widow), and former Gorbachev aide Alexander Yakovlev addressed a Moscow rally of 150,000 persons. Yeltsin barked back at the plotters, telling the crowd: "The junta that came to power will not stop at anything to keep that power. They understand that things have reached the point that if they lose, they will lose not only their armchairs, but they will be seated on court benches [as defendants]."[91] He spoke, however, for only ten minutes as snipers had earlier been seen in the vicinity.

Opposition flourished in other Soviet cities. In Leningrad Mayor Anatoly Sobchak addressed a rally of 200,000 protest-

ers, telling them never to yield to those trying to reestablish a dictatorship. *USA Today* reported that a crowd of 400,000 gathered in Kishinev, capital of Moldavia, and cried "Down with the dictatorship."[92] The nine Moldavian newspapers supporting the coup were ordered shut down by the local government.

In Belarus the Communist Party's Central Committee endorsed the coup, but the republic's Supreme Soviet, or Parliament, opposed it. The president of Kazakhstan also denounced the coup, and in the Ukraine eight thousand rallied to protest. The Ukrainian parliament condemned the revolt as illegal.

Meanwhile, in the Baltics, Estonia declared its independence. In response, Soviet troops poured into the country. One hundred armored vehicles rolled into Tallinn, Estonia's capital. In Latvia Soviet soldiers seized the republic's broadcast facilities and disarmed the prime minister's bodyguards.

Soon, however, it became evident that the plot had run out of steam. Military leaders met and agreed not to use force against the protesters. After first toeing the coup plotters' line, TASS, the official

Soviet news service, began issuing reports of opposition to the coup. Then, three of the eight coup leaders (Prime Minister Valentin Pavlov, Defense Minister Dmitri Yazov, and KGB leader Vladimir Kryuchkov) resigned from their posts.

The Return of Mikhail Gorbachev

By Wednesday, August 21, it was just about all over. Rumors spread that the coup leaders had fled Moscow. Tanks withdrew from the parliament area and from Moscow itself. Some Soviet troops began leaving the Baltics. Latvia joined Lithuania and Estonia in declaring its freedom.

The Soviet parliament voided all of the coup plotters' emergency decrees. As the coup collapsed, four of its leaders flew to the Crimea and apologized to Gorbachev. All were arrested, and former KGB chief Kryuchkov was brought back to Moscow in handcuffs.

President Bush spoke by phone with Gorbachev, who flew to Moscow and was met by guards sent from Boris Yeltsin's Russian republic's interior ministry. Yeltsin was clearly running the show.

By Thursday, August 22, all coup leaders had been arrested except for Interior Minister Boris Pugo, who had committed suicide in Moscow. An exhausted Mikhail Gorbachev spoke to the Soviet people on television: "Society must know, the entire world must know, what they were up to and what they wanted to do with me and what they wanted from me and did not get

The Whole of Society Had Changed

Soviet president Mikhail Gorbachev, in his book The August Coup: The Truth and the Lessons, *explained why the plotters failed:*

"If the coup d'etat had happened a year and a half or two years earlier it might, presumably, have succeeded. But now society was completely changed. The people who, five years previously, had been thirteen to fifteen years old were now eighteen or twenty. They had grown up in a different atmosphere. And they had become the most courageous defenders of democracy.

The whole of society had changed, including the Army that was part of it. Officers and privates refused to go against their own people despite the threat of court martial. The forces of law and order and even the special commando troops behaved similarly. That was where the plotters went wrong: they did not realize that society was now not what it had been a few years back."

In 1991 Russians show their support for Yeltsin over Gorbachev. The people had become frustrated with the continued economic troubles that Gorbachev seemed at a loss to solve.

from me. . . . I congratulate our Soviet people . . . for respecting all those to whom they entrust power."[93]

He also spoke of his gratitude for the support of old rivals such as Yeltsin: "We understood now what it was to be united. . . . We had in the past gone so far as to practically call each other enemies. And we began to think how . . . to pick up the pieces."[94]

Yeltsin, meanwhile, addressed a massive rally outside the Kremlin. One organizer asked the crowd how many thought Gorbachev should remain in power. They chanted "Resign! Resign!" Then he asked how many thought Gorbachev should remain "on vacation." Nearly everyone raised their hands. Later part of the crowd passed by the headquarters of the secret police, the KGB, and tried to tear down the statue of its founder, Felix Dzerzhinsky. They could not do it with ropes, but soon five giant cranes appeared and finished the job.

One of the supporters of the coup was the speaker of the parliament, Anatoly Lukyanov, a longtime close personal friend of Gorbachev. The betrayal deeply wounded Gorbachev. "Forty years bound us together; we had known each other since student days. . . . It's a tough lesson for me," *USA Today* reported him saying.[95] But Alexander Yakovlev expressed the view of many when he said that Gorbachev was to blame for the coup because he had surrounded himself with "a team of traitors."[96]

Gorbachev's initial reactions to the coup showed that he was out of touch with what was happening in the country. On his return to Moscow he acted as if nothing substantial had taken place, announcing his loyalty to the communist system and the Soviet Union. He then named a new lineup of hard-liners to replace the coup plotters. Public outcry was so great that they all resigned the next day.

On Friday, August 23, Gorbachev addressed the Russian parliament. He seemed totally dominated by Yeltsin. When Gorbachev made the point that some of his cabinet had not supported the coup, Yeltsin shoved a copy of a report on the coup to Gorbachev. "Read it!" Yeltsin demanded.

Russians ponder the downed statue of KGB founder Felix Dzerzhinsky. The secretive and powerful KGB, which had terrorized Soviet citizens, was finally at an end.

Meekly Gorbachev obeyed. Eighteen of his twenty ministers had been involved.

On Saturday, August 24, the Ukrainian parliament voted to secede from the Soviet Union. That same day Gorbachev dropped a bombshell, resigning as party leader and suggesting that the 400-member Communist Party Central Committee dissolve itself. He also authorized local governments to seize Communist Party property. By now, however, it was obvious that Mikhail Gorbachev, the architect of glasnost and perestroika, was more and more irrelevant to Soviet politics. "It would have been greatly to his advantage had he done this a year ago," commented Eduard Shevardnadze, "but now? It is too late."[97]

On August 26 Gorbachev continued his new, more flexible approach, allowing secession by the Soviet Union's republics. When the national Supreme Soviet voted 283 to 29, with 52 abstentions, to bar the Communist Party from all political activity and to freeze its assets, the Supreme Soviet stripped Gorbachev of his power to issue decrees concerning the Soviet economy. Gorbachev attempted to keep the Soviet Union from dissolving but it was increasingly apparent that he would not be able to succeed.

In the weeks that followed, the Soviet Union rapidly unraveled. Boris Yeltsin firmly controlled the Russian republic. One by one the other republics declared independence. Gorbachev was the president of a nation that no longer existed.

In December 1991 Gorbachev's power was further undercut when the Commonwealth of Independent States was formed. Eleven former Soviet republics (Azerbaijan, Armenia, Belarus, Kazakhstan, Kyrgyzstan, Moldavia, Russia, Tajikistan, Turkmenistan, Uzbekistan, and the Ukraine) joined this new non-Soviet federation.

On Christmas Day 1991 Mikhail Gorbachev, the leader who tried to save communism by reforming it, instead presided over its end. That day he resigned as president of the Soviet Union. It was effectively the death of the Soviet system.

Chapter

9 Beyond Gorbachev: Yeltsin and the Postcommunist Governments in Eastern Europe

The end of the Soviet system did not mean an end to Eastern Europe's troubles. Decades of economic mismanage-

Although the yoke of Soviet power had been broken, problems in the East bloc nations had just begun. A perilous waste dump in Czechoslovakia is emblematic of the dilapidated condition of many of the nations.

ment had left their mark. Widespread pollution endangered the environment. Inefficient enterprises closed, throwing those used to lifetime job security out of work. Prices, once rigidly controlled, rose dramatically. While some took advantage of new economic freedoms, most faced even greater difficulties than they had under communism.

The former Warsaw Pact nations confronted a variety of problems, including ethnic violence. Each country took a different approach and achieved different degrees of success.

Albania

Tiny, isolated Albania missed out on the revolutions of 1989. Until his death in 1985, Enver Hoxha, a hard-liner who never ceased to support the harsh policies of former Soviet dictator Stalin, ruled the nation. In 1961 he broke with the Soviet Union and allied himself with Mao Tse-tung's People's Republic of China. By 1978, however, Hoxha became displeased with Mao's revisionism and severed relations.

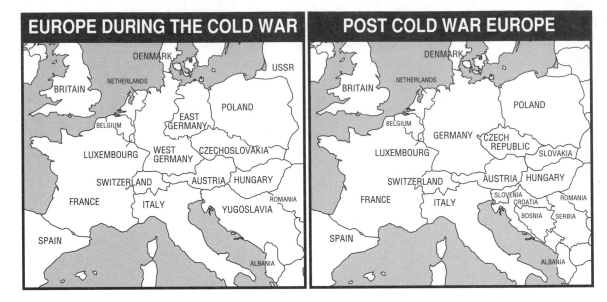

EUROPE DURING THE COLD WAR

DENMARK
USSR
NETHERLANDS
BRITAIN
POLAND
BELGIUM
EAST GERMANY
LUXEMBOURG
WEST GERMANY
CZECHOSLOVAKIA
SWITZERLAND
AUSTRIA
HUNGARY
FRANCE
ITALY
ROMANIA
YUGOSLAVIA
SPAIN
ALBANIA

POST COLD WAR EUROPE

DENMARK
NETHERLANDS
BRITAIN
POLAND
BELGIUM
GERMANY
CZECH REPUBLIC
LUXEMBOURG
SLOVAKIA
SWITZERLAND
AUSTRIA
HUNGARY
FRANCE
ITALY
SLOVENIA
CROATIA
ROMANIA
BOSNIA
SERBIA
SPAIN
ALBANIA

Under Hoxha's harsh rule not a single church or mosque remained open in the entire nation of 3.5 million people. For a time hermitlike Albania did not even have phone service with the outside world.

Some protests took place in 1989, but reforms did not actually start until 1990. Hoxha's successor, Ramiz Alia, ended Albania's bans on religion and foreign travel. Student riots broke out in the capital of Tiranë in December 1990, the students demanding opposition parties, and Albania's first such party, the Democratic Party, was formed. That month Albania tore down all remaining statues of Joseph Stalin.

Economic conditions, however, still worsened in what was already Europe's poorest nation. Thousands of Albanians fled, mostly to Greece and Italy. Alia won the April 1991 elections, but opponents alleged fraud. Strikes and violence swept the country as food shortages increased. The unemployment rate stood at 51 percent. Food production dropped by 56 percent.

Johanna Neuman quotes an Albanian newspaper editor in a *USA Today* article: "There is total poverty. We need investments so that we have something our country can rely on."[98] In June the Communist Party (known officially as the Party of Labor) changed its name to the Socialist Party and admitted other parties into a coalition government.

In March 1992 the Democratic Party's Sali Berisha became Albania's first noncommunist president, and Albania became the first former Warsaw Pact country to apply for NATO membership.

Bulgaria

In October 1991 a coalition of the Union of Democratic Forces and a party representing the country's Turkish minority replaced the former communists, who now called themselves socialists. In January 1992 Zhelyu Zhelev, an intellectual in the mold of Czechoslovakia's Vaclav Havel,

I Am Ashamed of My Country

The overthrow of the communist system did little to bring prosperity to Russia. Marshall Goldman in What Went Wrong with Perestroika *detailed many of the problems that remained. Many citizens shared the feelings excerpted here from Goldman's book of this fourteen-year-old Soviet high school student who wrote on February 14, 1991:*

"Last week I was standing in a terrible line for meat. Do you know how long I was standing there? I was even afraid to tell you, I was standing there for five and a half hours.

We had lines (as you know) [before] but they were not so big and we stood in those lines not for everything. But now we have lines for everything. Beginning with meat and shoes and ending with matches and salt. We stand for rice, for sugar, for butter, for thread, for deodorants, and . . . it is an endless list. You know I've forgotten the taste of 'Russian' cheese? It is not a joke. I'm serious, I really don't remember it.

Earlier I never cried. I have a strong character, but now I cry very often. We're becoming like animals. If you'd see our wild, mad and hungry people, in terrible and not less wild lines, you'd be in shock. Every country helps us. We already openly asked for alms and we accept them very calmly. We forget about one very good word. Pride. I am ashamed of my country."

Former Soviet citizens grab for food handouts after the collapse of the Soviet Union.

campaigned under the slogan "Democracy or Communism" and became president.

Bulgaria faced the usual problems: inflation, an 18 percent jobless rate in early 1994, and a foreign debt of eleven billion dollars (the equivalent of two years' wages for each Bulgarian). But postcommunist Bulgaria also had its positive aspects. Privatization of farms and businesses successfully took place, and the country's markets boasted plentiful food supplies.

The communists had persecuted the country's Turkish minority (about 7 percent of Bulgarians). They now fared much better; in one 1992 poll, 90 percent of them said they were pleased with Bulgaria's ethnic relations.

Czechoslovakia

Like Yugoslavia, modern Czechoslovakia was a multiethnic creation born of the treaties that ended World War I. On January 1, 1993, the urban Czechs and the more rural Slovaks peacefully went their separate ways, creating the Czech and Slovak Republics.

Before the breakup Czechoslovakia had been led by President Vaclav Havel. Havel was first elected in November 1989 and reelected in the spring of 1990. Rather than preside over his country's breakup, he resigned in July 1992. Czechoslovak economic policy had been formed by Vaclav Klaus, who first served as finance minister before becoming prime minister. Klaus was an admirer of British conservative Margaret Thatcher and believed in pushing his country toward a free economy. His program of "ownership through vouchers" led to a rapid transfer of enterprises to private ownership.

On January 26, 1993, Havel returned as president of the new Czech state. The Czech Republic enjoyed relatively good economic prospects. It boasted a trade surplus in 1993 and a low 3.5 percent un-

Vaclav Havel holds his nose against the putrid odor emanating from a mismanaged toxic waste dump in Prague. The environment was not a priority in the communist nations, where cleanups were simply unaffordable.

Although communism presented problems, citizens under its control were not challenged to find new ways to improve their situation. Left to her own devices, an East German woman searches a garbage container for useful items.

employment rate in early 1994. The Slovak Republic, on the other hand, faced not only high unemployment, inflation, and recession, but also ethnic problems. Eleven percent of its population was Hungarian.

East Germany

When the Soviet empire broke apart, many new nations were formed, but East Germany disappeared. In October 1990 the former German Democratic Republic (GDR) dissolved itself into five separate provinces, which then became part of West Germany. The reunited countries, now one Germany, are called the Federal Republic of Germany.

After reunification half of the old GDR's industrial workers were thrown out of work when inefficient state-run enterprises failed. Inflation in eastern Germany ran at 12.8 percent in 1991 and 11 percent in 1992. Balancing those difficulties were safety net programs provided by the far-

wealthier former West Germans.

Another problem facing eastern Germany was the continued presence of Russian troops on its territory—troops who had been there since Germany's defeat in World War II in 1945. The German government paid nine billion dollars to help in the removal of the troops by August 1994.

Hungary

On April 8, 1990, the conservative Hungarian Democratic Forum (HDF) in alliance with the Smallholders' Party and the Christian Democratic People's Party won Hungary's first free elections in four decades. The HDF's Jozsef Antall became prime minister. Arpad Goncz, a member of the rival Federation of Free Democratic Forum who had served six years in prison after the 1956 Hungarian uprising, was elected president. The new National Assembly declared October 23 a national holiday to mark Hungary's fight for freedom in 1956. In June 1990 Hungary left the Warsaw Pact, and all of the 73,500 Soviet troops occupying Hungary were gone by June 30, 1991.

Fifteen percent of the Hungarian economy had already been in private hands in 1989. The new government took a slow, cautious approach to increasing privatization and experienced relatively small drops in gross national product and increases in inflation and unemployment. Hungarians eagerly formed over ten thousand joint ventures with Western companies.

Poland

Poland made great progress toward private ownership after the communists left power but still faced harsh economic conditions.

After Lech Walesa captured the presidency, he appointed Jan Krysztof Bielecki to succeed Mazowiecki as prime minister. By July 1992 three others, including Hanna Suchocka (the first Polish female head of government) had served in that office. In May 1993 her six-party coalition was defeated in parliamentary elections.

Poland did achieve some progress. By December 1991, 45 percent of all jobs were in private enterprise. Private citizens controlled most retail establishments. Yet, even though the Polish economy grew by 4 percent in 1993, high inflation and unemployment continued.

Former Communist Party members, now called the Social Democrats, and their old allies, the Peasant Party took over in September 1993. Economic problems remained, however.

A Warsaw woman bemoans the huge price increases in market items. Polish citizens were not the only ones to find that the price of freedom was dear.

Romania

Romania was the only communist regime to be violently overthrown and to have its leader, Nicolae Ceausescu, executed. It was also the first to outlaw the Communist Party. Romania should have continued to move quickly away from its Marxist-Leninist past. Yet it became the first nation to elect a former member of the old communist leadership, Ion Iliescu, as president.

Former communists dominated Iliescu's National Salvation Front. In May 1990 Romanians gave Iliescu 85 percent of the vote in presidential elections. International observers said the vote was fair, but Iliescu's defeated opponents charged fraud. The following month in Bucharest, police attacked thousands of anti-Iliescu demonstrators. Iliescu brought busloads of miners into the city to intimidate the opposition. Four protesters were killed in the riots that followed. Hundreds were savagely beaten. Nonetheless, in the October 1992 elections Iliescu won 61 percent of the vote. This time irregularities were widely alleged. "As many Romanians say, there was a coup in December [1989]— not a revolution, because the old power structure remains the same," said Laszlo Tikos, professor of Slavic studies at the University of Massachusetts.[99]

Although there had been some movement toward private ownership and free speech, Romanians had little to show for the overthrow of the Ceausescus. In December 1993 inflation ran at 300 percent.

Unemployment stood at 10 percent. Strikes and government corruption sapped the nation's strength, and foreign investment was scarce. Ethnic hatred toward the Hungarian minority population increased. Romania, sometimes known as the "bread basket of the Balkans," imported food for the first time in 450 years.

Yugoslavia

Yugoslavia fared worse than any other nation after the breakup of Marxist-Leninist governments. Century-old ethnic and religious hatreds burst forth and caused hundreds of thousands of deaths. Serb forces seized territory from both Slovenia and Croatia when they declared independence. The international community imposed trade sanctions on Yugoslavia,

When Romanians chose to elect Ion Iliescu as president, they voted to continue communism—and many of its problems. Here, Romanian riot police chase demonstrators from outside Iliescu's palace in Bucharest.

Orphans in Sarajevo await evacuation from the war-torn city. In the former Yugoslavia, unchecked violence among ethnic minorities reigns at great human cost.

crippling Serbia's economy. Inflation reached 30,000 percent and two-thirds of the Serbs were unemployed.

In the Croatian-Serb conflict, Croatia lost one-third of its territory. The United Nations mediated a truce between Yugoslavia and Croatia in January 1992, but war soon broke out again. The Muslim-led Republic of Bosnia declared its independence. Bosnia's Catholic Croats formed the state of Herzeg-Bosna. Its Eastern Orthodox Serbs created a nation called Krajina. Although all sides committed atrocities, the Serbs drew the heaviest criticism for their brutal policy of "ethnic cleansing" (removing non-Serbs from contested areas)—a policy many said had degenerated into genocide.

By February 1994 the war in Bosnia had cost 200,000 dead and left 2 million homeless. Because of Serb and Croatian attacks, the central Bosnian government held only about one-fifth of the former republic.

The world was shocked in February 1994 when a 120 mm mortar shell landed in a Sarajevo marketplace, killing sixty-eight Muslim Bosnians and wounding almost two hundred. After NATO airstrikes the United Nations initiated a cease-fire in the area. A long-standing Russian sympathy for Serbia complicated the problem. If other nations took strong measures against Serbia, Russia might intervene on its side.

The independent republics that replaced the former Soviet Union all faced new problems: ethnic violence, inflation, unemployment, and the rise of ultranationalist leaders.

Here is what happened to some of the new nations of the old Soviet Union.

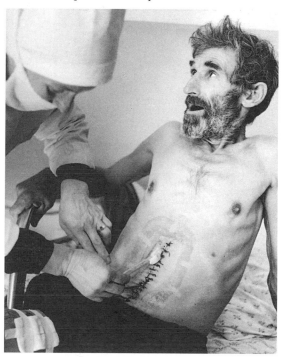

A Muslim man silently testifies to the senseless violence that is the result of ethnic hatred—he sits between the graves of his wife and daughter, both killed when mortar shells destroyed their apartment.

This Abkhazian man was wounded after Georgia declared independence in April 1990.

Lithuania

Lithuania, the first Soviet republic to declare independence, was also the first to vote former communists back into power. In November 1992 former communists, now operating as the Democratic Labor Party, under Algirdas Brazauskas defeated the nationalist *Sajudis* (Lithuanian Reform Party). Economic problems helped pave the way for the Democratic Labor Party victory, for in the first ten months of 1992 industrial output had fallen 48.5 percent.

Brazauskas was no old-line Marxist. He pledged to work for total Soviet troop withdrawal and kept his promise. In January 1994 Lithuania became the first of the former Soviet republics to apply for NATO membership and the first to enroll in NATO's Partnership for Peace program, a sort of junior partnership in NATO.

Ukraine

The Ukraine, with fifty-two million people and a reputation as the "bread basket of Europe," should have been a success story, but it was not. In December 1993 inflation ran at 100 percent a month. Heating fuel was scarce. Because of power shortages, television stations could stay on the air only from 6 P.M. to midnight. The government seemed unable to handle the economy and was widely regarded as corrupt. "Ukraine is not in a more difficult situation with regards to energy than the Baltics were in 1992 or Eastern Europe in 1990," said Duke University's Simon Johnson in a *U.S. News & World Report* article by Tim Meek. "All of them had to adjust. The difference is that Ukraine is refusing to adjust."[100]

The Ukraine still retained seventeen hundred Soviet nuclear missiles. Western nations wanted these weapons dismantled and offered the Ukraine $2.8 billion to do so. The Ukrainian parliament, however, was slow to agree to become a nonnuclear power.

After the Ukraine declared independence, it argued with Russia over control of the former Soviet Black Sea naval fleet. Ultimately the two nations resolved the problem. Another major point of conflict was the Crimea, a lush peninsula that since 1954 had been a part of the Ukraine. Seventy percent of its citizens, however, were ethnic Russians. In January 1994 a candidate favoring return of the area to Russia won the Crimea's presidency with 73 percent of the vote.

A Dangerous Moment

Because of food shortages, unemployment, and inflation, the future of freedom and market reforms in Russia was uncertain. In a Time *magazine interview, former Soviet foreign minister, Eduard Shevardnadze, now president of Georgia, was a pessimist:*

"The entire territory that used to constitute the Soviet Union is in a quagmire today. These countries have not had independence for a long, long time. Georgia was part of Russia for 2½ centuries, and now that it has started building a new independent society, it encounters many difficulties. We sometimes have a sense that there are no prospects. We have an economy that is absolutely ruined. Conflicts are raging in the former Soviet Union. In my opinion, these are not the last conflicts. Other conflicts are to be expected, and they will be on a larger scale. But I think the law of necessity will work; Abkhasians and Georgians, for example, have to live together. Even though this has been a tragic event with casualties, it will increase the responsibility of both sides."

In February 1994 the Ukraine became the first member of the Commonwealth of Independent States to join NATO's Partnership for Peace program.

Georgia

Violence swept Georgia after it declared independence in April 1990.

In 1991 former dissident Zviad Gamsakhurdia became president. Gamsakhurdia, however, grew increasingly dictatorial. Georgians ousted him in January 1992, and Eduard Shevardnadze became the new president.

In the fall of 1993 Gamsakhurdia led a rebellion against Shevardnadze. After being surrounded by progovernment forces in December 1993 Gamsakhurdia committed suicide.

Georgia also saw ethnic violence. In August 1992 fighting began in Abkhazia when that northwestern region of Georgia wanted to separate from the rest of the country. By 1994, 3,000 people there had died and 250,000 had become refugees.

Georgia was slow to join the Commonwealth of Independent States. In February 1994, however, Georgia signed a treaty allowing Russia to station troops on Georgian soil.

Armenia and Azerbaijan

Since 1988 Armenia and Azerbaijan had battled over the Nagorno-Karabakh region of Azerbaijan, a largely Armenian area. At first, the Muslim Azerbaijanis did well, but Christian Armenians won military victories

Demonstrators gather under a statue of Lenin in Azerbaijan.

in 1992 and 1993. They regained Nagorno-Karabakh and even captured 20 percent of the rest of Azerbaijan. Sixteen thousand had died in the conflict, and one million people lost their homes.

The war created energy problems for Armenia, which produced only 30 percent of its required electricity and which had previously relied on Azerbaijani oil. But since the breakup, these supplies were cut off.

Russia

Russian soldiers march in front of the parliament building on October 5th after fighting broke out between anti- and pro-Yeltsin hardliners.

Even after communism's collapse, the living standard of the Russian republic still declined. Conditions were so bad that between 1992 and 1993 life expectancy for Russian males dropped from 62 to 59. Such problems spelled trouble for President Boris Yeltsin's reforms. In September 1993 hard-liners in parliament impeached Yeltsin. He responded by dissolving that body and calling for December elections. The hard-liners, in turn, sparked fighting in the streets of Moscow, seizing the mayor's office and television facilities and announcing their intention to march on the Kremlin.

Living conditions continued to deteriorate in Russia after the communist collapse. Citizens faced long lines and empty shelves as food shortages plagued the nation.

I May Have to Shoot 100,000 People

Ultranationalist Vladimir Zhirinovsky, leader of the Liberal Democratic Party, captured nearly a quarter of the votes in Russia's December 1993 elections. His threats and wild statements alarmed many. Here is a sampling of his thoughts, as reported by the Associated Press on February 5, 1994:

"The Liberal Democratic Party stands for the restoration of the Russian state in the borders of the former U.S.S.R."

"I'll start by squeezing the Baltics and other small nations. I don't care if they are recognized by the U.N. I'm not going to invade them or anything. I'll bury radioactive waste along the Lithuanian border and put up powerful fans and blow the stuff across the border at night. I'll turn the fans off during the day. They'll all get radiation sickness. They'll die of it. When they either die out or get down on their knees, I'll stop it. I'm a dictator. What I'm going to do is bad, but it'll be good for Russia. The Slavs are going to get anything they want if I'm elected."

"I say it quite plainly: When I come to power, there will be a dictatorship. I will beat the Americans in space. I will surround the planet with our space stations so that they'll be scared of our space weapons. I don't care if they call me a fascist or a Nazi. Workers in Leningrad told me, 'Even if you wear five swastikas, we'll vote for you all the same. You promise a clear plan.' There's nothing like fear to make people work better. The stick, not the carrot. I'll do it all without tanks on the streets. Those who have to be arrested will be arrested quietly at night. I may have to shoot 100,000 people, but the other 300 million will live peacefully. I have the right to shoot these 100,000. I have this right as president."

On October 4 one thousand pro-Yeltsin soldiers stormed parliament. In a ten-hour battle they strafed the building with machine gun and tank fire, blasting huge holes in the side of the Russian White House and setting it afire. Three hundred died in two days of fighting before the hard-liners were crushed and order was restored.

The results of the December elections shocked the world. While a new constitution was passed that gave Yeltsin greater powers, ultranationalist Vladimir Zhirinovsky received as much as 23 percent of votes, and former Communist Party members got 25 percent. In February 1994 the new parliament pardoned the anti-Gorbachev coup plotters of August 1991. The reform process seemed threatened.

Mad Vlad

The rise of ultranationalist leader Vladimir Zhirinovsky alarmed many, both within and outside of Russia. Zhirinovsky's programs combined militaristic bluster, grand economic promises, racism, and anti-Semitism. He threatened Japan, Germany, Poland, and the Baltic states, and demanded the return of Alaska from the United States, which had purchased the area from Russia in 1867. He had supported the August 1991 coup against Mikhail Gorbachev. In his 1993 book *The Last Play for the South,* Zhirinovsky called for Russia to conquer Afghanistan, Iran, and Turkey.

Some, such as St. Petersburg's mayor Anatoly Sobchak, said that Zhirinovsky's Liberal Democratic Party (the first Russian noncommunist political party) was originally created by the Communist Party and the KGB. Others claimed that the million dollars he spent in his 1993 election campaign may have come from hidden East German Communist Party funds. In any case, the rise of such an irresponsible Russian leader was a frightening threat to world peace.

Vlad Zhirinovsky's extreme nationalist views seemed to threaten Russian reforms.

The Future

Predicting the future of the former Soviet bloc was not an easy task. Who in 1986 could have seen that the entire system would collapse in just a few years? And that it would do so with such little resistance from the ruling power structure? Or—except in Yugoslavia, Romania, and the Caucasus (Georgia, Armenia, Azerbaijan)—with so little bloodshed?

Unfortunately it was impossible to rule out further, even greater, violence or the return of tyranny under such leaders as Zhirinovsky. Still, the peoples of Eastern Europe made great advances toward freedom. The more freedom they knew, the harder it would be for potential dictators to fully turn back the clock and return to the closed system that once choked off all dissent and free speech.

"I am certain that my nineteen-year-old daughter and her generation will not face the kind of problems that have tormented us for many years," said one reformer, as quoted by Cohen and van den Heuvel. "It may be only that a truly free Soviet generation is only now beginning or isn't yet born. It is for them that we and perestroika [were] preparing the way."[101]

Notes

Introduction: A History of Distrust

1. Gilbert Seldes, *The Great Quotations.* New York: Pocket Books, 1976.
2. Mikhail Gorbachev, "Mikhail Gorbachev: My Final Hours," *Time,* May 11, 1992.

Chapter 1: The Establishment of Communism in Eastern Europe

3. Seldes, *The Great Quotations.*
4. Aleksandr Solzhenitsyn, *Lenin in Zurich.* Translated by H. T. Willetts. New York: Farrar, Straus and Giroux, 1976.
5. Brian Moynahan, *Comrades: 1917—Russia in Revolution.* Boston: Little, Brown, 1992.
6. Frank Alfred Golder, *Documents of Russian History, 1914–1917.* Translated by Emanual Aronsburg. Gloucester, MA: Peter Smith, 1964.
7. Seldes, *The Great Quotations.*
8. Basil Dmytryshyn, *U.S.S.R.: A Concise History.* New York: Charles Scribner's Sons, 1965.
9. Mikhail Heller and Aleksandr M. Nekrich, *Utopia in Power: The History of the Soviet Union from 1917 to the Present.* Translated by Phyllis B. Carlos. New York: Summit, 1986.
10. Heller and Nekrich, *Utopia in Power.*
11. Heller and Nekrich, *Utopia in Power.*
12. Dmytryshyn, *U.S.S.R.*
13. Heller and Nekrich, *Utopia in Power.*
14. Norman Davies, *God's Playground: A History of Poland; Volume II: 1795 to the Present.* New York: Columbia University Press, 1982.

Chapter 2: Everyday Life Under Communism

15. Eugene Lyons, *Workers' Paradise Lost.* New York: Paperback Library, 1967.
16. Hedrick Smith, *The New Russians.* New York: Random House, 1990.
17. Martha T. Moore, "Frontiers of Capitalism," *USA Today,* June 13, 1990.
18. Smith, *The New Russians.*
19. Hedrick Smith, *The Russians.* New York: Quadrangle, 1976.
20. Smith, *The Russians.*
21. Robert G. Kaiser, *The People and the Power.* New York: Washington Square Press, 1984.
22. *USA Today,* March 20, 1990.
23. Kaiser, *The People and the Power.*
24. Kaiser, *The People and the Power.*
25. Kaiser, *The People and the Power.*
26. Robert G. Kaiser, *Why Gorbachev Happened: His Triumphs and His Failure.* New York: Simon and Schuster, 1991.

Chapter 3: The First Signs of Rebellion

27. Reg Gadney, *Cry Hungary! Uprising 1956.* New York: Atheneum, 1986.
28. Harry Schwartz, *Prague's 200 Days: The Struggle for Democracy in Czechoslovakia.* New York: Praeger, 1969.
29. Quoted in Gadney, *Cry Hungary!*
30. Michel Salomon, *Prague Notebook: The Strangled Revolution.* Boston: Little, Brown, 1968.
31. Salomon, *Prague Notebook.*
32. Salomon, *Prague Notebook.*
33. Neal Ascherson, *The Polish August: The Self-Limiting Revolution.* New York: Viking, 1982.

34. Lyons, *Workers' Paradise Lost.*
35. Roland Gaucher, *Opposition in the U.S.S.R., 1917–1967.* Translated by Charles Lam Markham. New York: Funk and Wagnall's, 1969.

Chapter 4: Poland: Solidarity Defeated

36. Lawrence Wechsler, *Solidarity: Poland in the Season of Its Passion.* New York: Fireside, 1982.
37. Wechsler, *Solidarity.*
38. Mary Craig, *Lech Walesa and His Poland.* New York: Continuum, 1987.
39. Craig, *Lech Walesa.*
40. Wechsler, *Solidarity.*
41. Craig, *Lech Walesa.*
42. Craig, *Lech Walesa.*
43. Wechsler, *Solidarity.*
44. Wechsler, *Solidarity.*
45. Wechsler, *Solidarity.*
46. *Time,* "Man of the Year: Lech Walesa, He Dared to Hope," January 4, 1982.
47. Craig, *Lech Walesa.*

Chapter 5: The Rise of Mikhail Gorbachev

48. Stephen F. Cohen and Katrina vanden Heuvel, *Voices of Glasnost: Interviews with Gorbachev's Reformers.* New York: W. W. Norton, 1989.
49. Zhores A. Medvedev, *Andropov.* New York: W. W. Norton, 1983.
50. Thomas Butson, *Mikhail Gorbachev.* New York: Chelsea House, 1986.
51. Kaiser, *Why Gorbachev Happened.*
52. Kaiser, *Why Gorbachev Happened.*
53. Smith, *The New Russians.*
54. Kaiser, *Why Gorbachev Happened.*
55. Ronald Reagan, *An American Life: The Autobiography.* New York: Simon and Schuster, 1990.

56. Kaiser, *Why Gorbachev Happened.*
57. Butson, *Mikhail Gorbachev.*
58. Michael Kort, *Mikhail Gorbachev.* New York: Franklin Watts, 1990.

Chapter 6: Poland: Solidarity Triumphant Hungary: Goulash Socialism

59. Craig, *Lech Walesa.*
60. Craig, *Lech Walesa.*
61. Craig, *Lech Walesa.*
62. Craig, *Lech Walesa.*
63. Craig, *Lech Walesa.*
64. Carl Bernstein, "The Holy Alliance," *Time,* February 24, 1992.
65. Margarite Johnson, "An Epochal Shift," *Time,* August 28, 1989.
66. Charles Moritz, ed., "Tadeusz Mazowiecki," 1990 *Current Biography Yearbook.* New York: H. W. Wilson, 1991.
67. Michael Meyer, "Days of the Whirlwind," *Newsweek,* December 25, 1989.
68. Colleen Fitzpatrick, "Walesa Wins Polish Vote in Landslide," *USA Today,* December 10, 1990.
69. Peter S. Pritchard, "Walesa: 'If I Win, I Lose,'" *USA Today,* October 12, 1990.
70. Marshall I. Goldman, *What Went Wrong with Perestroika.* New York: W. W. Norton, 1991.
71. Stephen Smith and Michael Meyer, "Behind the Masks of Eastern Europe," *Newsweek,* October 16, 1989.

Chapter 7: The Rest of the Bloc Breaks Away

72. Reagan, *An American Life.*
73. Kaiser, *Why Gorbachev Happened.*
74. Russell Watson with Michael Meyer et al., "A Model Apparatchik," *Newsweek,* October 30, 1989.

75. Russell Watson with Michael Meyer et al., "A Model Apparatchik," *Newsweek*, October 30, 1989.

76. George J. Church, "Freedom!" *Time*, November 20, 1989.

77. Michael Meyer, "I Should Not Be Amazed—But I Am," *Newsweek*, January 1, 1990.

78. Moritz, *1990 Current Biography Yearbook*.

79. Moritz, *1990 Current Biography Yearbook*.

80. "Everything Can Change for the Better Now," *Newsweek*, December 25, 1989.

81. quoted by Strobe Talbott, "The Serbian Death Wish," *Time*, June 1, 1992.

Chapter 8: The Collapse of the Soviet Union

82. *USA Today*, August 26, 1991.

83. *USA Today*, July 13, 1990.

84. Boris Yeltsin, *Against the Grain: An Autobiography*. New York: Summit, 1990.

85. quoted by George J. Church, "Anatomy of a Coup," *Time*, September 2, 1991.

86. quoted by George J. Church, "Anatomy of a Coup," *Time*, September 2, 1991.

87. *USA Today*, August 23, 1991.

88. *USA Today*, August 19, 1991.

89. *USA Today*, August 19, 1991.

90. Bill Nichols, "'Yes' Man or Wily Hardliner?" *USA Today*, August 20, 1991.

91. Judy Keen, "'Keystone' Yeltsin Holds Opposition Together," *USA Today*, August 21, 1991.

92. *USA Today*, August 21, 1991.

93. Tom Savitieri, "'Healthy' Gorbachev Returns As Coup Fails," *USA Today*, August 22, 1991.

94. *USA Today*, August 23, 1991.

95. *USA Today*, August 28, 1991.

96. *USA Today*, August 22, 1991.

97. *Time*, September 2, 1991.

Chapter 9: Beyond Gorbachev: Yeltsin and the Postcommunist Governments in Eastern Europe

98. Johanna Neuman, "Albanians Expect Nation to Be 'More Beautiful, Happier,'" *USA Today*, June 26, 1991.

99. Marilyn Greene, "Romania's Day of Rage," *USA Today*, November 16, 1990.

100. Tim Meek with Douglas Stranglin, "Struggling to Keep the Flame Burning," *U.S. News & World Report*, December 20, 1993.

101. Cohen and vanden Heuvel, *Voices of Glasnost*.

Glossary

Baltic states: Lithuania, Latvia, and Estonia.

Bolshevism: Doctrine calling for the violent overthrow of capitalism; later became communism. Formed in 1903 when the Russian Social Democratic Party split into majority Bolshevik ("larger") and minority Menshevik ("less") factions.

capitalism: Economic system of private control of property.

COMECON (Council for Mutual Economic Assistance): Soviet-dominated international economic alliance; founded in January 1949.

Cominform (Bureau of Information of the Communists and Workers' Parties): Successor to the Comintern; founded in September 1947; dissolved in May 1956.

Comintern: Organization founded by Lenin in March 1919 to provide propaganda for and control of non-Soviet communist parties; formally dissolved by Stalin in May 1943.

communism: The political doctrine based on revolutionary Marxist socialism.

coup: Sudden overthrow of a government, by violence or the threat of violence.

czar: Autocratic monarch of Russia prior to 1917.

democracy: Government by the majority of the people acting in free elections.

five-year plans: Centralized economic plans first established by Stalin in 1928; emphasizes rapid growth in heavy industry and agriculture during a five-year period.

general secretary: From Stalin on, the highest office in the Communist Party of the Soviet Union (CPSU).

glasnost: Mikhail Gorbachev's policy of "publicity" or "openness" designed to begin free discussion in the Soviet Union.

Izvestiya **("News"):** Official Soviet government newspaper; at its peak *Izvestiya* had a circulation of 10.1 million.

KGB: The Soviet secret police; also known as the Cheka, OGPU, GUGB, NKVD, MGB, and MVD.

Kremlin: The complex of buildings housing the seat of both czarist and then Soviet power; located in Moscow.

Marshall Plan: Plan for post-World War II European economic recovery proposed by U.S. secretary of state George Marshall in June 1947; between 1948 and 1952 it provided $13.15 billion in aid for sixteen European nations.

Marxism-Leninism: Political, economic, and social principles of Soviet Marxism as interpreted by Lenin.

Mensheviks: Minority faction of Russian

Social Democratic Party (see Bolshevism); emphasized less conspiratorial and centralized tactics than the Bolsheviks.

NATO (North Atlantic Treaty Organization): U.S.-led military alliance, founded in April 1949 to prevent Soviet aggression.

Nazism: Brutal fascist ideology that ruled Germany from 1933 to 1945; also known as National Socialism.

Partnership for Peace: Auxiliary to NATO, designed after communism's collapse for former Warsaw Pact members.

perestroika: Gorbachev's "restructuring" of Soviet politics and economics, including multiparty elections and less centralized control of the economy.

Politburo: Ruling council of the former Communist Party of the Soviet Union (CPSU); members were chosen by the CPSU's Central Committee.

Stalinism: The policies of repressive Soviet dictator Joseph Stalin.

socialism: Social organization based on government control of the production and distribution of goods and services.

Solidarity: Polish labor union and social movement that led to the end of communism in that nation.

Supreme Soviet: The official Soviet legislature; composed of two houses: Soviet of Nationalities and Soviet of the Union; a rubber stamp for the CPSU.

totalitarianism: Political ideology calling for the domination of the individual person by the state and for all aspects of life to be controlled by the government.

Warsaw Pact (Warsaw Treaty Organization): Soviet-dominated military alliance founded in May 1955; dissolved as a military alliance on April 1, 1991.

For Further Exploration

William G. Andrews, *The Land and People of the Soviet Union*. New York: HarperCollins, 1991. This book covers not only the history but also the economy, culture, and ethnic groups of the Soviet Union.

Eleanor H. Ayer, *Boris Yeltsin: Man of the People*. New York: Dillon Press, 1992. A good summary of Yeltsin's career through the August 1991 coup.

Thomas Butson, *Mikhail Gorbachev*. New York: Chelsea House, 1986. This work suffers from being written very early in Gorbachev's leadership but presents a valuable overview of Soviet history.

Mary Craig, *Lech Walesa*. Milwaukee: Gareth Stevens Children's Books, 1988. A well-illustrated biography by an expert on Polish affairs. Aided by a useful glossary and time line.

Author's Note: The following films are available on video and are valuable for gaining a deeper insight into the Soviet experience.

Dr. Zhivago (1965), with Omar Sharif, Julie Christie, and Tom Courtenay; directed by David Lean. A classic telling of Boris Pasternak's novel of the Russian Revolution and the people caught up in it. The picture itself, Courtenay, and Lean were nominated for Oscars. Robert Bolt won an Oscar for the film's screenplay. Not rated.

The Inner Circle (1992), with Tom Hulce, Lolita Davidovich, and Bob Hoskins; directed by Andrei Konchalovsky. The story of a projectionist in the Kremlin during Stalin's rule. *The Inner Circle* shows something that is easy to forget—or that we find hard to believe—that many common people of the Soviet Union had a deep faith in Stalin even when they should have known better. Rated PG.

One Day in the Life of Ivan Denisovich (1971), with Tom Courtenay and Alfred Burke; directed by Casper Wrede. Excellent film of Aleksandr Solzhenitsyn's novel about a prisoner in the eighth year of his ten-year sentence to a slave labor prison camp. Denisovich's crime: escaping from a German prisoner-of-war camp during World War II.

Reds (1981), with Warren Beatty, Diane Keaton, Edward Herrmann, Jack Nicholson, and Maureen Stapleton; directed by Warren Beatty. The story of John Reed, an American journalist who was a sympathetic eyewitness to the Bolshevik Revolution. Overlong but still of interest. Most fascinating are interviews shown throughout the film of people who actually lived during that era. Actors Beatty, Keaton, and Nicholson and the picture itself were nominated for Academy Awards. Beatty won for best directing; Maureen Stapleton won for best supporting actress. Rated PG.

Stalin (1992), with Robert Duvall, Maximilian Schell, Joan Plowright, and Frank Finlay; directed by Ivan Passer. An HBO movie that chillingly captured the essence of Stalin's increasing paranoia and how it destroyed a widening circle of people around him. Filmed at some of the original sites of Stalin's life.

Works Consulted

Neal Ascherson, *The Polish August: The Self-Limiting Revolution*. New York: Viking, 1982. A journalist looks at the crushing of the Solidarity movement in 1981.

Carl Bernstein, "The Holy Alliance," *Time*, February 24, 1992. A lengthy cover story telling the remarkable story of U. S. and Vatican assistance to Poland's Solidarity movement.

The Book of Lech Walesa: A Collective Portrait by Solidarity Members and Friends. New York: Touchstone Books, 1982. The thoughts of those who knew Walesa during the period of Solidarity's rise.

Christopher Cerf and Marina Albee, eds., *Small Fires: Letters from the Soviet People to Ogonyok, 1987–1990*. New York: Summit, 1990. A fascinating collection of letters to a reformist magazine during the period of glasnost.

George J. Church, "Freedom!" *Time*, November 20, 1989. A lengthy but readable account of the breaching of the Berlin Wall.

Stephen F. Cohen and Katrina vanden Heuvel, *Voices of Glasnost: Interviews with Gorbachev's Reformers*. New York: W. W. Norton, 1989. Gorbachev was not alone in attempting to reform the U.S.S.R. An excellent collection of interviews with his close collaborators.

"Coup Leaders: No Strikes, No Rallies," *USA Today*, August 20, 1991. The text of an emergency decree by those who plotted the 1991 coup against Gorbachev.

Mary Craig, *Lech Walesa and His Poland*. New York: Continuum, 1987. Well-researched account of Walesa and the early history of Solidarity.

Norman Davies, *God's Playground: A History of Poland; Volume II: 1795 to the Present*. New York: Columbia University Press, 1984. An insightful and meticulously researched general history of Poland. Detailed and lengthy but very well written.

Louis de Robien, *The Diary of a Diplomat in Russia, 1917–1918*. Translated by Camilla Sykes. New York: Praeger, 1970. The memoirs of a youthful French diplomat in Russia during the revolution gives an eyewitness flavor to these events.

Basil Dmytryshyn, *U.S.S.R.: A Concise History*. New York: Charles Scribner's Sons, 1965. Somewhat dated but still valuable history of the Soviet Union.

"Everything Can Change for the Better Now," *Newsweek*, December 25, 1989. Article on the fall of Bulgarian communism.

Colleen Fitzpatrick, "Walesa Wins Polish Vote in Landslide," *USA Today,* December 10, 1990. Article on Walesa's winning the Polish presidency over his former friend Tadeusz Mazowiecki.

Reg Gadney, *Cry Hungary! Uprising 1956.* New York: Atheneum, 1986. A profusely illustrated, passionately told history of the Hungarian uprising.

Roland Gaucher, *Opposition in the U.S.S.R. 1917–1969.* Translated by Charles Lam Markham. New York: Funk and Wagnall's, 1969. A pioneering study of opposition to communism in the Soviet Union, including many little-known episodes.

Frank Alfred Golder, *Documents of Russian History, 1914–1917.* Translated by Emanuel Aronsberg. Gloucester, MA: Peter Smith, 1964. Exhaustive collection of primary documents relating to Russia during World War I.

Marshall I. Goldman, *What Went Wrong with Perestroika.* New York: W. W. Norton, 1991. A scholarly study of glasnost by one of America's foremost experts on Eastern Europe.

Mikhail Gorbachev, *The August Coup: The Truth and the Lessons.* New York: HarperCollins, 1991. Gorbachev gives his version of events in his usual bureaucratic style.

———, "Mikhail Gorbachev: My Final Hours," *Time,* May 11, 1992. An excerpt from Gorbachev's memoirs, detailing the end of his presidency.

Marilyn Greene, "Communism Crippled Health-Care System," *USA Today,* March 20, 1990. Details of shortages and shortcomings in Poland's health care system.

———, "Romania's Day of Rage," *USA Today,* November 16, 1990. Article concerning Ion Iliescu's crushing of Romanian protest.

Mikhail Heller and Aleksandr M. Nekrich, *Utopia in Power: The History of the Soviet Union from 1917 to the Present.* Translated by Phyllis B. Carlos. New York: Summit, 1986. Well-researched and well-written history of the Soviet Union, up to the Gorbachev era.

Jorg K. Hoesnch, *A History of Modern Hungary, 1867–1986.* London: Longman, 1984. A scholarly, short history of the Hungarian nation. Not as well written as Davies' history of Poland.

James O. Jackson with Frederick Ungeheuer and Egon Krenz, "Egon Krenz: He Stopped the Shooting," *Time,* December 11, 1989. Article about East Germany's Egon Krenz, including an interview with the former communist leader. The piece centers on Krenz's efforts to prevent bloodshed as the East German communist regime was crumbling.

Margarite Johnson, "An Epochal Shift," *Time,* August 28, 1989. Analysis of the forming of the noncommunist Solidarity government in 1989 Poland.

Robert G. Kaiser, *Russia: The People and the Power.* New York: Washington Square Press, 1984. A book similar to Hedrick Smith's *The Russians.* Both are highly recommended.

————, *Why Gorbachev Happened: His Triumphs and His Failure.* New York: Simon and Schuster, 1991. The respected *Washington Post* reporter offers thoughtful insights on Gorbachev and his political demise.

Michael Kort, *Mikhail Gorbachev.* New York: Franklin Watts, 1990. A useful short biography. Well illustrated.

Eugene Lyons, *Workers' Paradise Lost.* New York: Paperback Library, 1967. A well-organized and well-researched critique of Soviet communism. At the time Lyons's book may have seemed too harsh on the Soviet system, but recent revelations indicate that it was not.

Zhores A. Medvedev, *Andropov.* New York: W. W. Norton, 1983. A good short biography of the KGB leader by a veteran observer of the Soviet system.

Tim Meek with Douglas Stranglin, "Struggling to Keep the Flame Burning," *U.S. News & World Report,* December 20, 1993. An article detailing the severe difficulties faced by the new Ukrainian state.

Michael Meyer, "Days of the Whirlwind," *Newsweek,* December 25, 1989. Analysis of the split between Walesa and Mazowiecki shortly after Solidarity became politically powerful in Poland.

————, "I Should Not Be Amazed—But I Am," *Newsweek,* January 1, 1990. A brief interview with Czech dissident Vaclav Havel.

Martha T. Moore, "Frontiers of Capitalism," *USA Today,* June 13, 1990. Article detailing the problems confronting would-be capitalists in postcommunist Poland.

Charles Moritz ed., *1990 Current Biography Yearbook.* New York: H. W. Wilson, 1991. A reference collection of solid short biographical articles.

Brian Moynahan, *Comrades: 1917—Russia in Revolution.* Boston: Little, Brown, 1992. A popular account of the Russian Revolution of 1917. Good background on events leading up to the Bolshevik takeover.

Johanna Neuman, "Albanians Expect Nation to Be 'More Beautiful, Happier,'" *USA Today,* June 26, 1991. Article concerning optimism in formerly isolated, but still highly troubled, Albania.

Peter S. Pritchard, "Walesa: 'If I Win, I Lose,'" *USA Today,* October 12, 1990. Short article telling of Lech Walesa's concerns on the eve of his assuming the Polish presidency.

Boris Pyadyshev, *Russia and the World: New Views on Russian Foreign Policy.* New

York: Birch Lane, 1991. Russia's new leaders speak out on foreign policy—including some surprisingly restrained views from Vladimir Zhirinovsky.

Ronald Reagan, *An American Life: The Autobiography*. New York: Simon and Schuster, 1990. The memoirs of the American president whose term saw the cold war coming to an end. Useful for that perspective and for his thoughts on Gorbachev.

Michel Salomon, *Prague Notebook: The Strangled Revolution*. Boston: Little, Brown, 1968. A journalist stationed in Prague gives his version of Dubcek's rise and fall.

Thomas A. Sancton, "Man of the Year: Lech Walesa; He Dared to Hope," *Time,* January 4, 1982. A detailed look at Walesa written while he was still in prison following General Jaruzelski's December 1981 crackdown.

Harry Schwartz, *Prague's 200 Days: The Struggle for Democracy in Czechoslovakia*. New York: Praeger, 1969. Another telling of the events of the Prague Spring. More scholarly than Michel Salomon's account.

Gilbert Seldes, *The Great Quotations*. New York: Pocket Books, 1976. A standard collection of historical quotations.

Eduard Shevardnadze, "The Dark Forces Are Growing," *Time,* October 5, 1992. A pessimistic interview with the former Soviet foreign minister, which proved to be unfortunately accurate about Russia's immediate future.

Grazyna Sikorska, *A Martyr for the Truth*. Grand Rapids, MI: William D. Eerdmans Publishing, 1985. The story of Father Jerzy Popieluszko as told by a supporter of the Solidarity movement.

Hedrick Smith, *The New Russians*. New York: Random House, 1990. An updating of Smith's previous work, *The Russians,* consistent with the author's high standards.

———, *The Russians*. New York: Quadrangle, 1976. A classic explanation of life under the communist system by a respected *New York Times* reporter. Lengthy but well worth reading.

Stephen Smith and Michael Meyer, "Behind the Masks of Eastern Europe," *Newsweek,* October 16, 1989. Interviews not only with Hungary's Imre Pozsgay but also with other East European leaders.

Jill Smolowe, "East Germany: Trading Places," *Time,* October 30, 1989. Account of the turmoil preceding the end of East German communism.

Vladimir Solovyov and Elena Klepikova, *Boris Yeltsin: A Political Biography*. New York: G. P. Putnam's Sons, 1992. The authors stoutly defend Yeltsin and his program.

Aleksandr Solzhenitsyn, *Lenin in Zurich*. Translated by H. T. Willetts. New York:

Farrar, Straus and Giroux, 1976. Solzhenitsyn gives his fictional version of Lenin's time in exile. One of Solzhenitsyn's more accessible works.

Strobe Talbott, "The Serbian Death Wish," *Time,* June 1, 1992. Talbott, who would later become President Clinton's secretary of state, looks at a crumbling Yugoslavia.

Leon Trotsky, *The History of the Russian Revolution.* Translated by Max Eastman. Ann Arbor: University of Michigan Press, 1957. A classic account by one of those closest to the center of events.

Russell Watson with Michael Meyer et al., "A Model Apparatchik," *Newsweek,* October 30, 1989. A profile of East Germany's Egon Krenz.

Lawrence Wechsler, *Solidarity: Poland in the Season of Its Passion.* New York: Fireside, 1982. An American journalist looks at the Solidarity experience from the viewpoint of one involved with the American trade union movement.

Boris Yeltsin, *Against the Grain: An Autobiography.* New York: Summit, 1990. Yeltsin's own story, told in the blunt manner that won him popular support.

Index

Picture Credits

Cover photo by Reuters/Bettmann

AP/Wide World Photos, 19, 27, 35, 57, 60(bottom), 75, 79(top), 84, 89, 92, 95, 96, 108(both)

Archive Photos, 13, 39, 40(both), 41(both), 42, 82

Archive Photos/Archive France, 45

The Bettmann Archive, 15, 17, 18, 20(top)

EASTFOTO, 73(bottom), 74

J. L. Hamar/Archive Photos, 25

ITAR-TASS/SOVFOTO, 21, 31, 56, 60(top), 86, 105(bottom)

Mark H. Milstein/EASTFOTO, 105(top)

MTI/EASTFOTO, 36

National Archives, 22, 24

PAP/EASTFOTO, 67

Reuters/Bettmann, 11, 28, 33, 34, 43, 48, 52, 61, 63, 65, 68, 70, 71, 73(top), 78, 79(bottom), 80, 81, 85, 87, 90, 93, 97, 99, 100, 101, 102, 103, 104, 107, 110

RIA-NOVOSTI/SOVFOTO, 12, 62(top)

UPI/Bettmann, 10, 20(bottom), 38, 47, 49, 54, 62(bottom), 72, 77

About the Author

David Pietrusza has written for numerous publications including *Modern Age, The Journal of Social & Political Studies, Academic Reviewer,* and *The New Oxford Review.* For two years he produced the nationally syndicated radio program, *National Perspectives.*

Mr. Pietrusza has also written extensively on the subject of baseball. He is the president of the Society for American Baseball Research (SABR) and associate editor of *Total Baseball.* His three books on baseball are *Lights On!, Major Leagues,* and *Baseball's Canadian-American League.* He lives with his wife, Patricia, in Scotia, New York.